CAT-DEPENDENT NO MORE

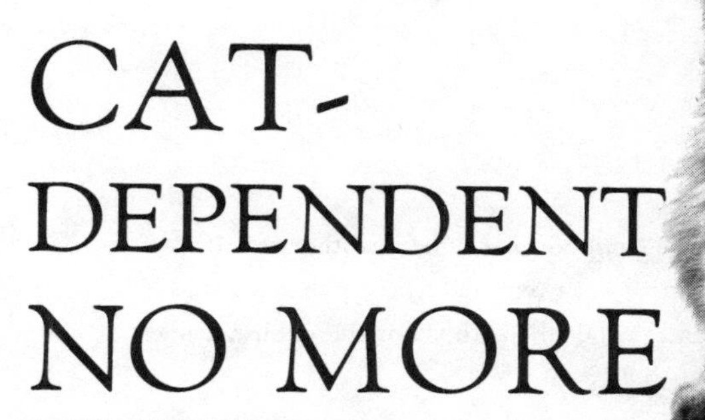

CAT-DEPENDENT NO MORE

Learning to Live Cat-Free in a Cat-Filled World

"DR." JEFF REID

FAWCETT COLUMBINE
NEW YORK

A Fawcett Columbine Book
Published by Ballantine Books
 Published in the United States by Ballantine Books, a division of Random House, Inc., New York, and simultaneously in Canada by Random House of Canada Limited, Toronto.

Library of Congress Catalog Card Number: 91-75881
ISBN: 0-449-90668-X

Cover design by Dale Fiorillo
Cover photograph by Walter Chandoha
Text design by Beth Tondreau Design

Manufactured in the United States of America
First Edition: January 1992
10 9 8 7 6 5 4 3 2 1

CONTENTS

FOREWORD

Redundancy is the key to information.
—INFORMATION THEORY TRUISM

Repetition works, as they say in advertising, and it works overtime in the self-help realm. Those who have tried to help themselves at the wellness smorgasbord of popular nonfiction will know this truth first-hand. And no one knows it better than "Dr." Jeff Reid, who has penned a number of these desultory volumes (*What Color Is Your Kitten?*, *The Purrsuaders*, and *A Fur, Fur Bitter Thing*). It seems that self-help authors live by their own "Three Rs": repeating, recycling, and repeating.

Judged by prevailing literary standards, of course, self-help books can be cynically described as derivative, self-indulgent pap that insults even the dubious intelligence of the American breeding public (and recent achievement tests find college bound freshmen routinely bested by rhesus monkeys). Standards have sunk so low, as one wag put it, that today's best-sellers are yesteryear's best-cellars.

Yet is there some method to this badness? When I first encountered "Dr." Reid's work I had my doubts. The prose was sloppy, repetitive, and profoundly obvious. The tone was all folksy chatter sprinkled with psycho-babble. As I absorbed the material, however, I found that in some curious way the psycho-babble was alchemically transmuted into psycho-baubles—semiprecious gems of pop psychology.

Eventually, I came to hear an echo of this holistic approach in my own related clinical work (see, especially, *Claw of Desire: Quadruped Parameters of Urban Contemporary Emotional Experience*). Reid demonstrates with his pet problem what every researcher knows—oftentimes the direct route through a field of study is a shortcut to nowhere.

Also seemingly problematic yet ultimately appropriate was Reid's strategy of skipping from topic to topic. The narrative, such as it was, leapt around like a crazy cat—ricochetting from sofa to chair to Tiffany lamp. Suddenly it hit me! (Not the lamp, but the power of Reid's "shaggy cat story.") This approach really *is* metaphorically apt for the person whose attention span has been shattered by living with an out-of-control cat. Considered in this light, *Cat-Dependent No More*'s rambling, mobius-strip form is a psychological perfect fit.

Moreover, Reid has avoided making *Cat-Dependent No More* too academic—he knows that the mental fog comes in on little cat footnotes. To further this user-friendliness, the text is sprinkled with helpful diagrams and illustrations.

I've heard it said somewhere that redundancy is the key to information. If that's so, I can assure you that after

Shelf Help for Any Ailment

reading *Cat-Dependent No More*, you will be loaded with key information. But of course, whether you actually wise up is another matter—a topic "Dr." Reid says he hopes to address in the sequel.

—Dr. Deedee Rigueur, Ph.D.

INTRODUCTION

When I first considered writing *Cat-Dependent No More: Learning to Live Cat-Free in a Cat-Filled World*, my initial thought was, "Where to begin?" Perhaps, I naively hypothesized, begin with the beginning, follow thereupon with the middle, and conclude, bam-boom, with the ending.

Then came the nagging doubts, what I like to call "the warm scuzzies," those familiar auto-harassment feedback loops that are as perversely comforting as they are dysfunctional. In my self-interrogation, I wondered if I should surrender so early to the baleful linearity that fouls so much "science." Why give in to the oppressive narrative dogma of "beginning-middle-end"? And yet, as the Chinese proverb has it, "The greatest journey begins with a single step." Similarly, this book, and the epochal notion of cat-dependency, began with a simple typographical transposition—the step from "pets" to "pest."

Such is the kind of happy accident that leads down the royalty-laden path to wellness. Or, at least, what-the-hellness. In any case, I think I'm getting ahead of myself. But isn't that always just the way? It seems that in the burgeoning realm of personal growth, you're always getting ahead of yourself. And paradoxically, your improved self is always just up ahead leading you unconsciously to the new and better "you" that's always right there in front of yourself if only you'd grab on to it. Always.

After such a heady mental prelude of interior counterpoint, my higher power (my editor, that is) suggested that perhaps it would be best to begin with a rambling personal anecdote. Ah, just so. Because this scientific foray is also a transformational personal odyssey.

Chapter One

THE CULT OF THE NONEXPERT

The cat owner can't smell the box, but that doesn't mean it doesn't stink.

—SUPPORT-GROUP SLOGAN

I'm no expert, but I play one on TV. You may have seen me on the chat-show circuit talking about my cat-dependency workshops, yet I'm no more of an expert than you are. If I appear more knowledgeable it may only be because I know more—a cognitive advantage gained through an acquired experience differential.

Despite my non-expert status, however, people often ask me, "What is cat-dependence? Who has it and why? What are the symptoms? Is it contagious? Could I have it and not know it?"

I say, "Whoah!" Or as some say in the counselling industry, "Hold on a second." If we answer all those questions at once, confusion may result. "Right away is right awry," as the recovery slogan goes—meaning that changes quickly made are just as quickly unmade. Moreover, if we cover (or recover) too much ground too quickly it won't be much of a book, will it? And although I'm no expert, just an ordinary person like yourself, I *have* amassed some small expertise in the course of writing several books on various feline domestic disorders.

EASY DOESN'T

Luckily for me, cat-dependency is an amorphous concept that defies easy definition. Even within the counselling field, debates rage as to whether cat dependency is a disease or just a dis-ease. Some maintain that all cat owners are to some degree cat-dependent; in effect, any relationship with a cat is unhealthy. Others believe that healthy cohabitation, that is, cat-habitation, is possible in theory if difficult in practice. There is even a rancorous dispute in clinical circles about the movement's nomenclature, i.e., should it be referred to as "cat-dependence" or "cat-dependency"? It is, as we say in the field, "all academic." (See especially, *Cat-Dependence or Cat-Dependency: A Submerging Issue* by C. Ibid and E. G. Frinstanz et al.).

It certainly seems that when it comes to cat-dependency, the only thing certain is uncertainty. In any case, cat-dependence, whatever it may be, is closely connected to the booming co-dependency cottage industry. (Co-dependency is that constellation of interrelated syndromes in which the personality is deformed by close proximity to aberrant significant others. These "others" are often chemically dependent, or fat, or lazy, or disinclined to perform household chores. Or something. And the co-dependent, or insignificant other, tends to make excuses for the true malefactor's bad behavior—to the point of totally distorting his or her own life.)

Like co-dependency, cat-dependency is the "sickness" of the "well" partner. Obviously, by analogy, cat-dependency is the condition whereby a person distorts his or her life by extreme emotional fealty to a feline. And, as often happens with the mates of alcoholics, the cat-dependent person covers up the problem, takes the blame, makes excuses, denies there's a problem, and enables the problem to continue—thereby ensuring that the problem gets worse.

Like a smoker, or someone who dates lawyers, the cat-dependent person exists in a cognitively dissonant state of perpetual denial. The cat-dependent person may know unconsciously that what he or she is doing is dangerous or wrong, yet no evidence will dissuade him or her from the path of cuddly self-destruction (the dozens of cat-borne diseases, the damaged property, the damaged lives.)

These cat lovers may love unwisely, but they can rationalize like any neglected lover. We hear their plaintive voices: chewing off the phone cord is a cry for help, destroying a computer is a cry for help, playing poop hockey is a cry for help, coughing up hairballs is a cry for help. Actually, of course, it is this type of lame rationalization that is a cry for help. But that doesn't mean it doesn't hurt. (In other words, that does mean that it does hurt.) Consider this heartfelt missive from the cat-dependent trenches:

> Dear "Dr." Reid,
>
> I've tried everything I can think of, but it just doesn't add up. Twelve steps to sobriety, eleven paths to enlightenment, ten to your own business (as well as going the whole nine yards and eight ways to breakfast). I've heeded the seven deadly warning signs, read about the six sure-fire ways to six figures in the coming recession, worked my way through the five stages of the grieving process. For kicks, I tried three ways to look out for #1. Yet after all that, my cat still makes me feel like a big zero. What's a girl to do?
>
> Anita Partridge
> Peartree, Vermont

I told Ms. Partridge that although she's done everything by the numbers, that doesn't count for much these days.

Well Rounded Individual	Cat Dependent (pulled in many directions)	Shredded Personality (advanced stage of Cat Dependence)

Unfortunately, there's more than numerology involved in kicking the kitty habit. If you need help, I've got some numbers for you: 1-900-976-CatD (there is a $10 processing fee per call in addition to the per-minute rate, but you get what you pay for—this skimpy little paperback book you're reading is a bargain at only $5.99, yet it'll only take you so far. Call now for more personal attention—phone-screening para-therapy professionals are waiting to take your call).

EMOTE CONTROL

A cat-dependent person often finds it difficult to give up "control" of their cat's life in cases where both pet and master are obviously out of control. And even in the best of situations, the cat-dependent's vision of control is a hallucination.

If your significant other is alcoholic, at least you can urge him or her into treatment for alcoholism. But what is the treatment for felinism? In any Twelve-Step program for cats, four of those steps will likely be in the litter box. And it's tough enough to get a cat to go into the other room, let alone to attend a Twelve-Step-program meeting.

To extend the analogy, few drunks ever reform themselves, but even fewer are reformed by others. And the odds for cat reform are worse—yet their only hope is for their nominal owners to release them into the realm of their own personal responsibility. (Moreover, the whole concept of "reform" is cosmologically dubious. In order to "re" form anything you must be capable of forming it in the first place—a creative generative leap obviously still beyond the best genetic engineers, let alone the lowly cat-dependent.) Cat-dependency is further complicated by the fact that it's a hybrid syndrome with the worst aspects of dependency and co-dependency, i.e., in some ways, cat-dependence is an addiction and in others it resembles an addiction to another person's addiction-distorted life.

Yet whatever the difficulties of defining the parameters of cat-dependence, most experts would agree that this dysfunction, or "network of not-working behaviors" as we like to say, mostly afflicts outwardly "well-adjusted" individuals with plenty of disposable income and free time. People like "you."

This isn't to suggest that our counselling is just "con" and "selling" with "u" stuck in it. No, far from it, though many of you do get stuck in counselling. And of course, many wellness outreach facilitators *are* money-grubbing charlatans—their outreach is for your wallet and the sooner they can facilitate it, the better.

The dangers, ironically and then some, were elucidated by my former colleague and co-author Dr. Peter Astor (DDS) in the preface he penned for our book *Women Who*

Love Cats Too Much. "No problem? No problem," he wrote. "Because no problem is too insignificant to write a profitable self-help book about." Astor's no-problem dictum proved problematic for me and we parted ways shortly thereafter. (Those interested in a fuller treatment of this therapeutic schism can peruse my article in the dependency journal, *That All Depends*, entitled, "Co-Written No More: Exorcizing the Ghostwriter in the Machine.")

EMOTIONAL CHECKPOINT/ HANDY CHECKLIST

As you can doubtless tell already, everything having to do with cat-dependency is steeped in controversy or simmering in anger (if not stewing in its own juices). So if experts can't agree on cat-dependency, you shouldn't worry about not grasping the concept in its entirety right away. You should, however, know how you feel. You should always check your feelings, but never check them at the door.

Do you feel:

- ☐ Anxious
- ☐ Eager
- ☐ Agitated
- ☐ Uptight
- ☐ Wired
- ☐ Stressed out

Good. Welcome to the human race. There's nothing wrong with feeling that way. In fact, there would probably be something wrong with you if you thought everything was all right. Take a deep breath and move on to the next chapter.

Chapter Two

PETS AND MASTERS—WHO'S WHO?

Let sleeping dogs lie, but wake up those lying cats.

—CATALONIAN PROVERB

We all know people in thrall to their cats—they pamper them, pander to their whims, and praise their independence. It all seems rather harmless. And it is—for the felines. For the "masters," however, this apparently harmless bond can become emotional slavery. The cats remain essentially wild animals with the run of the house, while their owners are curiously corralled. We've all heard the rationales, the excuses, the alibis, the synonyms.

"Shamus punted his little poopies out of the litter box, up the stairs, and into my purse—he must be cross with me."

"Nefertiti gnawed off my shoelaces again. . . . I must be neglecting her."

"Sebastian really likes you! It's not every dinner guest whose plate he'll jump onto and wave his anus in their face."

Aye, there's the rub. Up close and impersonal. And yet, sufferers of the syndrome insist that their own manifestations of it are as unique and beautiful as snowflakes. Each individual sees the profound nuances of his or her own pet problem without glimpsing the all-encompassing (or "big") picture. It's sometimes difficult, as a therapist, to avoid bone weariness—when so many flakes are piling up, one can get tired and cold from the shoveling.

Consider a few more of these excruciatingly exquisite permutations:

MOLLY'S FOLLY—
OLIVER, WHY NOT TAKE ALL OF HER?

"My cat Oliver's bad behavior is really a sort of prescience," according to Molly, a director of television commercials. "When I first dated Tim, Oliver would drag Tim's jackets into the corner and urinate on them. Tim was really a crybaby. He was totally pissy about it. Or sometimes after Tim and I would make love, Oliver would mess the bed. When Tim and I broke up I could tell that Oliver, for all his muted insolence, had been tapping into a higher level of awareness about Tim. He was really into a sixth sense or something—cats have this uncanny ability to read people. Now all my boyfriends have to pass the Oliver Test."

MICHELLE'S HELL—
LIVING WITH THE NAMELESS ONE

"Sure I get angry sometimes," says Michelle, a self-effacing social worker with intense brown eyes. "But it's not really his fault that my cat never learned cat-box etiquette—

he never even learned his name. I know I'm to blame for that. When I first got him from my mom as a kitten I named him Lawrence of Suburbia. But then I began calling him Lawrence, then El Awrence, and then Larry, L-O-S, Los(s), Burbs, Subby . . . Discipline became difficult, to say the least. It's hardly surprising that he misbehaved, given all the different names I called him when I punished him for various indiscretions. It's also not surprising that he ultimately became known as Sybil, the cat with multiple personalities—all of them bad."

JEAN'S SCENE—
THE RAT RACE AND THE CAT CHASE

"Isis only acts up when I neglect her—like when I'm gone all day at work, or if I go out at night, or if I read a book in the bedroom," says Jean, a meek, zoftig secretary. "It's a small apartment to leave her stranded in. I'd like to get her a larger place. But to advance at the office (in order to earn more so as to afford more space) I have to work longer hours, which means I neglect her more. It's a vicious circle."

Indeed. And sometimes, that circle can become a downward spiral that leads to a person opting out of life. In extreme cases, these manipulated "masters" show symptoms strikingly similar to agoraphobia—this hybrid cat-dependent syndrome is known as angoraphobia and it can get quite hairy. Let's take a closer look at one such sufferer.

SALLY'S RIDE

Sally, an attractive, intelligent woman and a secretary at a big Chicago law firm, is a typical case. She suffered from a marginal deficiency in region-specific social skills, i.e.,

Some Early Warning Signs of Cat Dependence

A weekend in Hawaii sounds great, but I don't Know if I can find anyone to cat-sit.

When I first dated Mary everything was great. But my cat Sabrina bristled and I felt she was attuned to a deeper level of awareness. I broke it off with Mary.

He only humps your shoes and gnaws your laces because he likes you. He's indifferent to everyone else.

indifference to the feats, fates, and fetes of Cubs, Bulls, Bears, and Sox. As a sports-trivia washout, svelte Sally found herself alone too many nights until she finally cracked. Some turn to alcohol for warmth and solace, but not Sally. When her self-esteem suffered, she retreated to the tenuous emotional security of the beast.

As often happens, it started innocently enough. But nights of kitty cuddling and TV watching led to more serious matters. Sally was quickly succumbing to the modern malady of cocooning. In an age of video shopping networks, cable TV, home computers, video movie rentals, and other stay-home inducements, it becomes easier than ever to withdraw into an isolated fantasy land. Sally became one of many to spin an electronic cocoon that starts out cozy and ends up feeling like an emotional coffin.

Soon, Sally would hesitate to leave the house for any reason. At first it was just on the weekends, but eventually she began calling in sick to work, preferring her cat's company. Soon her company was preferring a new secretary, while she went through a rigorous daily regimen of squeaker-toy aerobics and Tom and Jerry reruns.

Happily, Sally has been steered back toward sanity, thanks to joint intervention by myself and the local animal cruelty authorities (cat-dependency sometimes endangers pet as well as master; the term "smothered with affection" can be more than a metaphor).

We also enlisted the aid of specialist Dr. Rich Pettybone, an outreach facilitator coordinating various interfacing wellness consortiums and clearinghouses. Pettybone, along with the animal-protection authorities and myself, designed a workable program for Sally that involved getting the "kitten off her back" through behavioral modification. Behavior Mod is a highly complex system that involves the modification of behavior. Among the high-tech tools we used in this case were polysyllabic jargon, federal matching funds, starched white lab coats and albino rats. Not to mention some nifty graphs and beakers. We also utilized a form of aversion therapy, which Sally didn't really take to—but that's another story.

ANOTHER STORY

As I noted above, a version of aversion therapy was tried with Sally in which images of her "demon kitty" were linked to her sports loathing. This was done in tandem with drug therapy aimed at inducing nausea when her thoughts turned to things feline. The nausea-inducing drug in this instance was a widely used imported ethanol preparation. Unfortunately, we got our wires crossed and Sally initially developed an aversion to the therapy.

Instead of the intended effect of linking feline aversion with sporting contempt, the Brewskies (the generic name for the drug we used) created a "euphoric appreciation of mindless physical contests," (to quote one researcher). In other words, Sally became a sports fan—another potentially dangerous dependence. But that's yet another story, if not another book.

Suffice it to say that the esoteric program of behavior modification mentioned above largely succeeded in modifying Sally's behavior. (Though she still often has outbursts of hysterical tears whenever she watches the Northwestern Wildcats play football, it is unclear whether she is having cat-dependent flashbacks or is merely a football fan.)

Some Later Warning Signs of Cat Dependence

I need to get a larger apartment; this place is too confining for my cat Caesar.

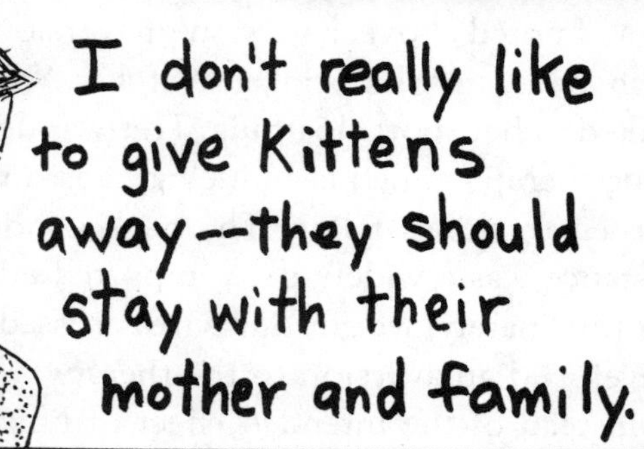

I Know it's a little drastic for a 15-year-old cat, but I think Sam deserves a $40,000 liver transplant.

Sally's ride wasn't an easy one, and it's not over yet, but with perseverance and an understanding support group, she's controlling her cat-dependence.

ACTIVITY

Overcoming cat-dependence, or any other problem for that matter, requires some personal working through. Below are some activities that will help you cope with the complicated problem that is cat-dependency. Don't be frustrated if you can't successfully achieve all of these things right away. Remember: "Right away is right awry," as they always say in support groups. Licking cat-dependency is a laborious process, not a glorious end in itself.

- ☐ Take an inventory
- ☐ Make a list
- ☐ Tally your emotions
- ☐ Total your feelings
- ☐ Sum up your experience
- ☐ Add to your understanding
- ☐ Tax yourself
- ☐ List your personal inventory
- ☐ Divide your attention
- ☐ Categorize your priorities
- ☐ Prioritize your categories
- ☐ Go back and check your work
- ☐ Feel your real emotions
- ☐ Feel your fake emotions
- ☐ Experience the totality
- ☐ "Work-through" recognition
- ☐ Recognize your work

- ☐ Work toward "through-ness"
- ☐ Validate your emotions
- ☐ Validate your parking
- ☐ Figure out who's been naughty and nice, but keep it to yourself
- ☐ Quest for excellence
- ☐ Excel at questing
- ☐ Facilitate affirmations
- ☐ Affirm yourself
- ☐ Affirm your thighs
- ☐ If line 7 is greater, this is REFUND DUE YOU

Chapter Three

ALLEY CATS OR ALLY CATS: "MY" STORY

A cat has nine lives, how about you?

—CAT-DEPENDENCY SLOGAN

In the course of my travels promoting my cat-dependency seminars, cat "lovers" often accost me in a hostile mode. They're mad enough to scratch my eyes out! "You monster," one typically shrieked, "how can you castigate my Thorstein so?" Or another reproach: "I wuv my widdo Jenkins-poo, why does the mean old man say such naughty fings about him?" Sometimes, too frequently, they bring their beloveds along—as if to help convince me that "to know know know him is to love love love him."

Often as not at my post-seminar coffee klatches the fur begins to fly (both feline and "human"). Cat jumps cat, master jumps master, cat jumps master—every permutation imaginable. And most of the time, it's the humans who are much the worse for wear. After the fur has settled, the rationalizations start to fly: "Charlemange was only defend-

Cat Dependence...it gives one paws
Progressive Breakdown of Self

ing himself." "Jezebel was in heat." "Himmler was just following orders."

Yet despite this nearly inevitable fracas, I keep my cool. I understand. Because I, too, was once in thrall to an indifferent furball. I was seriously cat-dependent. Indeed, I still am a recovering cat-dependent, because recovery is a costly lifelong process. Perhaps you'd like to hear my story. Rest assured that every word is true.

It wasn't the tale that grew in the telling.

It was me.

"MY" STORY

I was in college when I recognized I had a problem with my cat, Trevor. It wasn't until years later, however, that I came to realize that the root of my problems with Trevor stemmed from my parents' relationships to their cats. Mom and Dad had two cats and two children, but it was difficult to tell which mattered more to them. Mom was a "clean freak" bordering on "neat-aholic" and everything my sister and I did seemed to "mess everything up," to use mom's incessant description. The house was so clean that we could not only eat off the floor, but we were often forced to because Mom was worried about us "messing up" the tablecloth.

Moreover, we were never allowed into the living room, which was a shrine to Mother's tawdry taste and anti-lint predilection. Her ceramic owl collection couldn't have been any neater or cleaner had it been sealed in plastic (like the couch, chairs, and lamps.) The cats, Minnie and Max, were given the run of the house—they could often be found nestled into the plasticoated settee in the living room sharpening their claws and shedding hair like there was no tomorrow. Ironically, it was my sister and I who took the blame for this: "If you kids would quit pestering those cats," my mother would always say, "they wouldn't be wreaking so much havoc in 'my room.' "

And my father wasn't any help. He could always be found down in his "wrecked room" (as he called it), puttering with his tool—a needle-nosed pliers. Withdrawn as he was, however, he did have a knack. He could build or repair just about anything with wire coat hangers. (Once he made a working model of the solar system for one of my school projects using only bent coat hangers and some cracked Ping-Pong balls).

I finally realized that my mother was cat-dependent and my father was co-cat-dependent. But it was tough to get them to therapy, to say the least. (But I'm not the kind to just say the least, as you well know by now. You've got to "get it out" or your toxic feelings will corrode your inner life. There are also dire "environmental consequences" to turning friends and family into emotional toxic waste dumps—but more on that another time.)

My mother was resistant to the idea of visiting a counsellor because therapy, no matter what, is always messy. My dad was in denial and, wouldn't you just know, denied it. He didn't even see that he had a problem until the mid-'80s when the proliferation of plastic hangers left him short of materials and therefore long on time to contemplate his conundrum. It nearly drove him crazy, but he stopped short of insanity by seeking professional help.

THE OLD COLLEGE TRITE

As is often the case (I would later learn), my personal cat-dependency crisis was precipitated by external pressures (just as my father's would later be). I was a typically deluded sufferer of a syndrome that was still nameless at this point. I thought that in my personal life I was maintaining well, rotating steaming pots of stress from front burner to back like a master chef. Instead, I was unwittingly intent on preparing a multi-course mental breakdown. School, romance, and family pressures were part of my recipe for disaster—but the main ingredient was Trevor (though like others afflicted by the mental illness of cat-dependency, I was loathe to admit it. It's no coincidence after all that the word "can't" contains the word "cat").

I was in the midst of my second attempt at Sociology 101—one of those notoriously tough college courses intended to weed out the weaker specimens. It was a grind, but it laid the groundwork for the development of cat-dependency theory. We were forced to memorize all of the standard deviations, and several that I considered substandard. We gleaned how quibbles are quantified, and determined methods of methodizing methodologies. We charted the differences between self-actualizing behavior and actual self-izing behavior (something I hadn't imagined was possible, let alone necessary).

We learned, for instance, that different people (and peoples) had different ways of viewing the world, what we would later learn to call their "world views" (and, after a bit of graduate school, we might even—in a similar but more sophisticated vein—wield the unwieldy "Weltanschauung"). Central to our extensive reading list were *The Bell Curve* by Sylvia Graph and *The Man Who Mistook His Wife for a Cat* by Olivoil Snaks.

Though I had trouble passing the class the first time, on the second go-round my professor recognized that I "had the gift for the obvious," and gave me high marks. It was his encouragement and critique that helped me pinpoint Trevor as the central core root of my basic essential problem.

TREVOR'S TALE

Trevor was a bushy-tailed tomcat who did what he wanted, when he wanted, where he wanted. His father was a neighborhood calico Casanova, his mother a high-strung Siamese kitten machine. I rationalized that given this "street" background, Trevor's antisocial actions were natural. He was prone to violent mood swings, which I somehow attributed to my behavior. The extra hours I spent studying were somehow really malign neglect on my part. His "love bites" and slashing claw marks were my well-earned comeuppance. By my warped reckoning, shredded stereo speakers and gnawed-off coaxial cables were fair compensation for a weekend away.

(I would later realize that I knew more about my cat's temperament than my sister's. To my chagrin, it turned out my sister preferred it that way, but we're still working through those issues in family therapy.)

Trevor's independent spirit appealed to me for obvious reasons—whereas he was a laissez-faire feline, I was chained to my social responsibilities. When he drove people away from me, I blamed them—or myself. My then-girlfriend Sheila is a case in point. Whenever she'd stay over at my apartment, Trevor would terrorize her—sometimes subtly, sometimes not. A favorite tactic of Trevor's was to wait until we went to bed and then creep up on the headboard—just above Sheila—and lurk there. He almost never pounced, but poised as a living sword of Damocles, Trevor exacerbated Sheila's insomnia. That, and his habit of spraying her purse and shoes, served as the catalyst for a romantic meltdown.

At the time I didn't take Sheila's complaints about the cat seriously. I pathetically defended Trevor, asserting that Sheila was just trying to blame her problems on a helpless animal. Such was my irrationality back then that I didn't even see the irony in this—it was actually my refusal to blame this "helpless animal" that was incapacitating me and destroying my relationship.

Needless to say (but what the heck, I'll say it anyway) after our breakup my schoolwork started to suffer. And hours lost mooning over mangled love meant less time for appeasing Trevor. As Trevor forced friends and acquain-

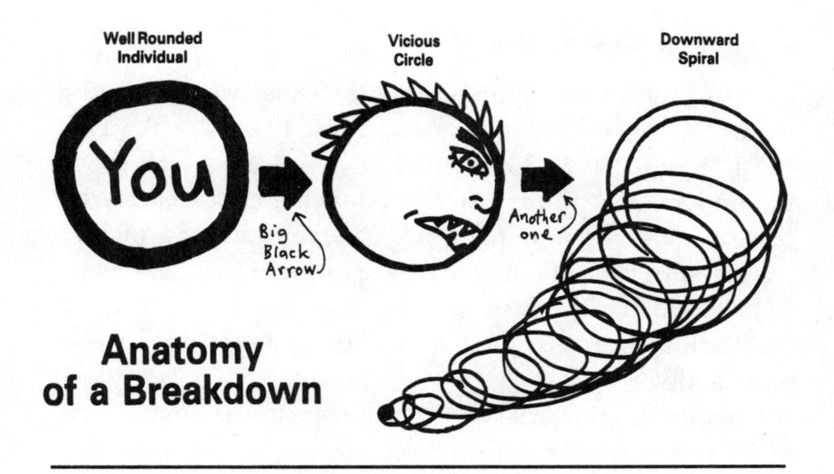

tances out of my life he became more belligerent, nearly driving me crazy (which by this time wasn't much of a commute). My lucrative position as part of an experimental control group for the psychology department was jeopardized because I was increasingly out of control. What began as a mood swing threatened to leave me literally swinging from the rafters.

Everybody has a moment of truth and mine came during my suicide attempt. It's difficult to convey the asphyxiating sense of claustrophobia that my responsibilities induced. As I threw the rope up over my dorm-room chandelier to facilitate my hanging, Trevor began playing with the tangled mass of hemp like it was just a harmless ball of string, not the grisly harbinger of my impending death. *Ah, the innocent pleasures of being a natural creature*, I mused.

Resigned to my impure fate and anticipating the blessed peace death would bring, I stood on a chair, tied a noose around my neck, and kicked the chair out from underneath me. As I felt myself slipping into the other world, Trevor began batting at my shoelaces and feet LIKE I WAS HIS LITTLE PLAYTHING. My ire began to rise as I kicked out in annoyance at the frantically pouncing cat, even as the cord cut deeper into my neck, thereby choking off my oxygen supply. Suddenly, my wave of futile anger gave way to that golden warmth people always describe when they're on death's doorstep. I felt myself rising up even as I was sinking down.

I awoke, anything but dead, with rope burns on my neck and a mangled light fixture beside me.

I was a tad befuddled but I was sure that the glow from the other side wasn't just some asphyxiation-induced hallucination. The vision that stayed with me was strong: as I hung twisting slowly in the wind, Trevor viewed me as just another dangling ball of yarn.

From that moment, I was on the rocky road to recovery. I had moved from Denial to Anger—I wanted to kill that damned cat! I knew instinctively that escaping from what I would soon dub "cat-dependency" would be difficult. But I resolved that if I could make it back from the other side, I would help others do the same—no matter what the price. Anyway, I figured they'd be willing to pay.

Chapter Four

CLASS ACTS AND CAT-DEPENDENTS

If all the cats in the world were laid end to end, it would be a good thing.

—ANGRY CAT-DEPENDENT

After I made my breakthrough (literal and figurative), I worked out the mechanics of my system in a seminal seminar entitled, "How to How-to." This seminar, headed by the well-known researcher Arty Kunst, was nothing if not practical (and, to be fair, not a few found it to be nothing). For those who "got it," however, the nuts-and-bolts orientation was a godsend. Rather than dwell in the sterile, clinical world of research, this "breeder-reactor"-type master class was geared toward "production" of books and seminars. For a semester project, each student was required to produce a coherent self-help system and present it to the class.

The class always attracted a variety of freethinkers and fast-buck artists (not to mention some fast-buck artisans, and, in the '70s, a few fast-buck craftspersons). This interest was understandable, because the seminar had launched quite a few minor self-help "hits" such as *Men Who Don't*

Flush and the Women Who Nag Them To as well as *Addicted to Self-Help: The "Problem" Problem*, and of course, the seminal *Denial of Depth—Five Steps to a Smoother Psyche*.

UNIFIED FIELD THEORY OF DEPENDENCE

A promising avenue of study in our class was explored by Carla Marcusson, one of a handful of student researchers working on a Unified Field Theory of Dependence. This may seem a little bit off the track of cat-dependency, but sometimes the long way home is the only way to get there. I think you'll find that it's worth the trip. It's a *process*. Getting there is not only half the fun, it's also the whole point.

Marcusson noted that all kinds of dependence—whether on drugs, approval, work, food, or mates with dependencies—were strikingly similar in the morphology of their addictive structures. Moreover, she asserted, they all bore an uncanny resemblance to the basic transactions sanctioned and celebrated by our commercially oriented society.

I can't say that I fully understood Marcusson's system, but I took extensive notes. What follows is roughly what she said in her presentation to the class. (Those interested solely in cat-dependence could skip ahead to the next section, but Marcusson's system has more than passing relevance.)

According to Marcusson:

"One had longings, which, if they couldn't actually be satisfied, could at least be momentarily assuaged by a purchase of some sort. You can't always get what you want, but you can always get *something*. Yet every transaction becomes hollower than the last—unless you up the ante.

After the elation of purchase comes the saturnine ebb of withdrawal (sometimes mistakenly diagnosed as 'payment dread'). To stave off this depression generally requires another, larger purchase. Money changes everything, but mostly it just changes hands.

"My Unified Field Theory of Dependence," she continued, "links macro and microeconomics as well as pop and mass psychology in what can be termed 'a four dementia manifold of chaotic equilibrium.'

"Under Keynesian economics, markets must endlessly expand or the whole economy will collapse. And something similar is at work in the personal realm. People expand their social horizons to keep their well-being in the growth mode—thereby staving off a personal collapse. And just as our government and huge corporations focus only on the short term—quarterly profits, pork-barrel politics—so, too, do individuals favor the quick-fix solution to their personal problems. ("I know John treats me badly, but it's the only attention I can get"; "I may have a hangover tomorrow, but it's not tomorrow yet—if I drink enough, maybe it will never be tomorrow.")

SHELF-HELP AND OUR SICK SOCIETY

As a corollary to her theory, Marcusson viewed pop psychology and self-help books as "just another deformation of the American psyche." While she allowed the validity of the personal-growth impulse—if so many people think they're sick, we probably are (as a society)—Marcusson and her cohorts saw the self-help explosion as a perversion of the natural will to self-improvement, which was exploited as a mere market niche. Middle-class people nervous about such things as "the bomb" or their place in the corporate hierarchy were transformed into anxious pop-psychology consumers.

Marcusson argued that the *New! Improved!* self proffered by so many best-selling authors is just one more example of highly successful planned obsolescence. In other words, self-help books offer such weak medicine for what ails us that repeated applications are needed (i.e., a new best-selling syndrome every eighteen weeks).

The class was duly impressed by Marcusson's critique, and our professor praised the analysis. Yet he wondered aloud, "Where's the money in *that*?" To which she replied, "Everywhere—haven't you been paying attention?"

Yipes! I thought, for I was then a college student, prone to such puerile internal exclamations. Marcusson's elaborate theory put mine to shame. All I'd come up with so far was a system for overcoming existential dread and paralysis by taking responsibility for your own actions, recognizing your cosmic insignificance, and treating others with respect. That just wouldn't wash. I made an appointment to visit Kunst in his cubbyhole during office hours.

I met him later that day. We talked for a few minutes about my life and the problems I foresaw with my proposed self-help presentation. When I told Kunst the rough outline of my system, he said:

"Sartre imitates life."

"But I don't follow."

"Doesn't surprise me," he said. "What you've got here is some warmed-over existentialism. That and seventy-five cents will get you on the bus. If you want to transfer for downtown, you'll need some Nietzsche or Whitehead."

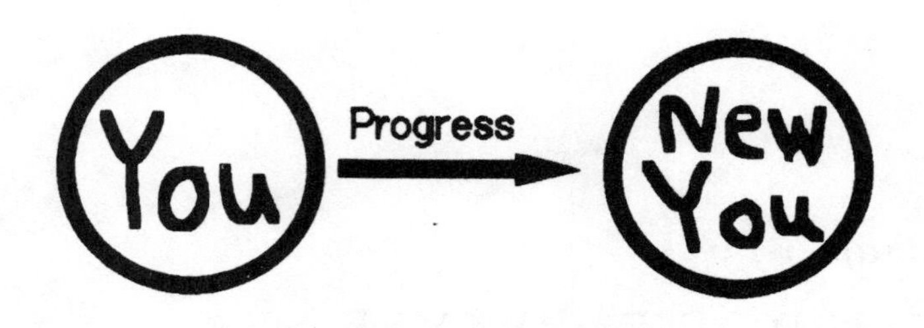

When I tried to elaborate on what I was getting at he interrupted again. "You've been having some troubles at home, isn't that right?"

Befuddled (I supposed he meant my botched suicide attempt), I nodded a waffling assent.

"Just as I thought," he said. "Pussy-whipped. Ninety-nine times out of one hundred that's what existentialism boils down to: problems stemming from pussy."

He offered me a consoling nip from the bottle of Jack Daniel's that he pulled from his bottom desk drawer.

I took it. Any port in the storm. Or any whiskey.

Suddenly it hit me, not the Jack, but what had been eating at me. It was indeed pussy, specifically Trevor. My head was swimming. Maybe it was just Jack taking over, but it felt like a whole lot more. In a sort of trance I excused myself, made my way home and got to work. In my mind I could already see it taking shape: cat-dependence.

The whole system poured out of me in one huge cathartic upheaval that night. The first thing I did the next morning was put the cat out. For good. The rest is history. For more information, see my early works: *Concatenation: America Hooked at Home*; *The Boy Who Washed His Cat Too Much*; and especially, *The Boy Who Put His Cat in the Microwave*. But enough about me. It's time to get back to your problems with cat-dependence.

Chapter Five

SUPPORT GROUPS: ONE MAN'S CRUTCHES ARE ANOTHER MAN'S STILTS

Support groups are really really really
important.

—SUPPORT-GROUP SAYING

When I began, there were no cat-dependency support groups as such, there were only fellow sufferers. Often these sufferers were dealing with grief as well as loss so it was a tough row to hoe. It was a complex situation. The subtle distinction between grief and loss always threw me for a loop. (Also, as an added complication, I wasn't sure if the saying was "a tough row to hoe" or "a tough road to hoe.")

So we started an impromptu coffee klatch-support group to zero in on common issues that we held in common as well as other shared group experiences and commonalties. We all talked about our cats, though I was the only one to do so in any systematic way. I was testing out my theories in the laboratory of life.

We would meet each week at my apartment to work through some issues. After we finished with the magazines we got down to business. Just hearing others' problems and their similarities to mine was helpful inasmuch as ideas sometimes resonated through the entire group. This would often continue for hours until the neighbors started pounding on the walls, complaining about all that resonating.

Sometimes people would read something that had moved them. One time, Charlie read his eviction notice. Sharon read an inspirational aphorism from Norman Vincent Repeal: "All ye who shall, so shall he who." It was food for thought, that's for sure. Or at least junk food for thought.

GETTING IT ALL OUT—THE DEEP SICKS

Eventually and invariably, though, Phil would start talking about his dear departed cat Sabrina and everyone would start reaching deep down inside themselves. If you've ever reached down deep inside yourself or others, you know that what comes up is not always a pretty sight. What we dredged up at those meetings was pretty ugly, if you'll pardon the oxymoron, but we all shared it and that made it bearable.

I told of how I sometimes missed Trevor, even though I had chosen to put him out of my life. I know it sounds crazy, but sometimes I felt like I needed a shot of chaos—and Trevor was always good for that. The other group members listened and didn't judge. They knew how judgmental that might seem.

Then each of them took their turn. Karen waxed nostalgic for her little puffball's mad slashing attacks on the curtains. It gave her a sense of purpose, however skewed, to ward off these strafing runs. And now they were no more, leaving her with a peculiar emptiness. But it was *her* emptiness and she fully owned it. Owning your emptiness was far better than renting, though some preferred to lease. All in all Karen understood that it was better this way. "Don't be an enabler; be an enobler," she intoned, repeating one of our group's favorite catch phrases. But every catch phrase has a catch, as each of us well knew. And there was another bittersweet truth imbedded within that one: Where there's a catch, there's a cat.

Of course we all instinctively knew that "putting out the cat" is never easy. It was just one of those unspoken truths. In a similar kind of synchronistic solidarity, we would often find ourselves humming that portion of the Flintstones theme song where the lyrics go: "Someday maybe Fred will win the fight, then that cat will stay out for the night." It seemed oddly fitting to us that there was never actually a cat on the program—it struck us as just another instance of the cultural denial of cat-dependence.

Nonetheless, some in my group were surprised to find that cats can damage the fabric of family life as easily as they can shred a sofa cushion. And often the cat's "owner" doesn't realize that other family members' lives have been distorted by living in a cat-dysfunctional home. Listen to the voice of Jennifer, whose mother sought therapy for cat-dependence yet left the family at home to deal with their own loss and dislocation.

"It seemed that at first, Mom cared more for that cat than she ever did for us. It was a drag to be ignored by your mom

From Cat, a tonic, to catatonic

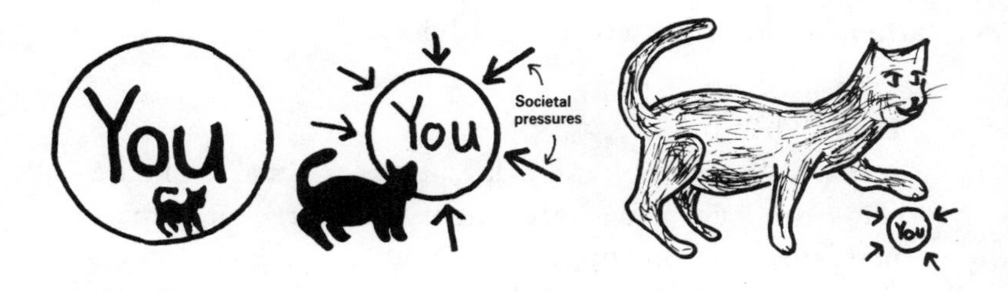

over a measly little cat, which nobody really liked in the first place. But it got even worse after that. She started ignoring us in favor of her therapy. So first it was the cat, and then it was the absence of the cat that took our mother away. It's gotten so I just don't feel anything anymore."

In many similar instances, cat owners and their families unwittingly make this psychic trip from "cat, a tonic, to catatonic."

One thing is for certain, though, after the cat departs, you've got to learn to feel your own feelings, the ones you've been suppressing, the ones the cat's been acting out. *You* can be angry. *You* can be cute and cuddly. *You* can rub up against people's legs.

Getting in touch is a long process, one that most people aren't ready for. People can't believe their cat is the problem in the first place, and after Fluffy departs, they can't believe their pet is responsible for the emotional black hole they are feeling. Cat dependents always have to remember to:

"Forget felis domesticus and just feel us."

But of course that's sometimes more difficult than it

sounds. Consider the plight of this reader of one of my earlier books, who wrote for advice.

> Dear "Dr." Reid,
>
> Everywhere I look these days, there are images of cute cats—on coffee mugs, greeting cards, refrigerator magnets, even suction-cupped to Toyota Corolla windows. I don't mean to whine, but this is very tough on a recovering cat-dependent person such as I find myself to be. Isn't there anything we can do to protect ourselves from this onslaught?
>
> I am especially troubled by the comic-strip schizophrenia exhibited by one of these beasts (which to avoid legal entanglements we might call "Scarfield"). This well known fat cat seethes with malevolence all week long like a typically poisonous specimen, but Sunday's full-color comic is always some heartwarming homily that ends in a hug. These Sunday strips are invariably the ones that end up attached by magnet to refrigerators across the land. What can be done about these media mixed messages?
>
> Rattled in Racine

"Rattled's" plight is typical, which is not to say trivial. And she touches, however obliquely, on a potential solution to this problem: legal action. I have a team of lawyers already at work on a class-action lawsuit that would recover damages from cartoonists and others who promote unrealistic stereotypes of cat behavior. If you'd like to join in what promises to be a huge (and hugely profitable) class-action suit, call 1-900-976-CatD.

ACTIVITY

The letter from "Rattled in Racine" raised a good point about the pervasiveness of misleading cat imagery. Stop and think of all the places cat images appear. The cute cat industry makes an estimated $7 billion per year. Buy a notebook and keep a journal of all the blatant and subliminal cat-vertisements you see. Below are a few to start your list.

- ☐ T-Shirts
- ☐ Calendars
- ☐ Cartoon books
- ☐ Sunglasses
- ☐ Refrigerator magnets
- ☐ Edible underwear
- ☐ Sporting-event blimp endorsements
- ☐ Tattoo royalties

Chapter Six

THE ROAD TO RECOVERY: WHAT WE'RE DRIVING AT

Always start with a quote.

—TERM-PAPER TRUISM

Even though many men are stricken with cat-dependency, it remains largely a female malady. If dog is man's best friend, then cat is woman's. But like any friendship, it must be a two-way street, as Sally Rand and Steve MacNally state in their pathbreaking book, *Friendship: A Two-Way Street*. "Friendship," they write, "must be a two-way street."

But is this cat/woman thru-way a two-way?

I would suggest, in fact, am suggesting, that it is, in effect, not. Indeed, this road well trammelled is an emotional one-way—feelings are steered by the woman toward a cavalier feline with nothing coming back the other way. Sadly, this emotional one-way also proves to be a dead-end street.

But just as lost drivers adamantly deny their predicament, those who find themselves pointed down a cat-dependent cul-de-sac often insist that they know what they're doing, thank you, and they wouldn't be there if they didn't want to be. This transparent false bravado is a warning sign of things going out of control.

You can see the traditional five steps of the grieving process come into view like dangerous curves as these cranky travelers drive themselves to the brink. Be patient with them: what they're grieving is the death of their relationship with their cat—and they don't even know it. First in the five-step process, as we have seen, there's denial, followed swiftly by anger ("You know so much, *you* drive"). Next comes bargaining ("Well, which way do you think we should go—maybe you were right all along"). After that there's depression about the fact that there's no detailed road map through the emotional wasteland of modern life ("You mean we're just relationships that pass in the night?"). Finally, there is acceptance, and then and only then can the lost soul be steered to a safe haven by the trained professional.

If someone you know is heading down this dangerous road, you've got to help them slam on the brakes. You might try to help them recognize their disorientation by giving them a copy of this book. But coming on too strong can be a mistake. Don't alienate them with harangues about their cat-dependence, no matter how well-founded your evidence. Often, the best route is to broach the subject gingerly once or twice, but when progress isn't forthcoming withdraw and seek professional help.

But rest assured that if they break down on the road of life, we'll tow them to a safe haven. Peace of mind demands peace and quiet, and we understand that people need a combination of AA and AAA. We've found that a sup-

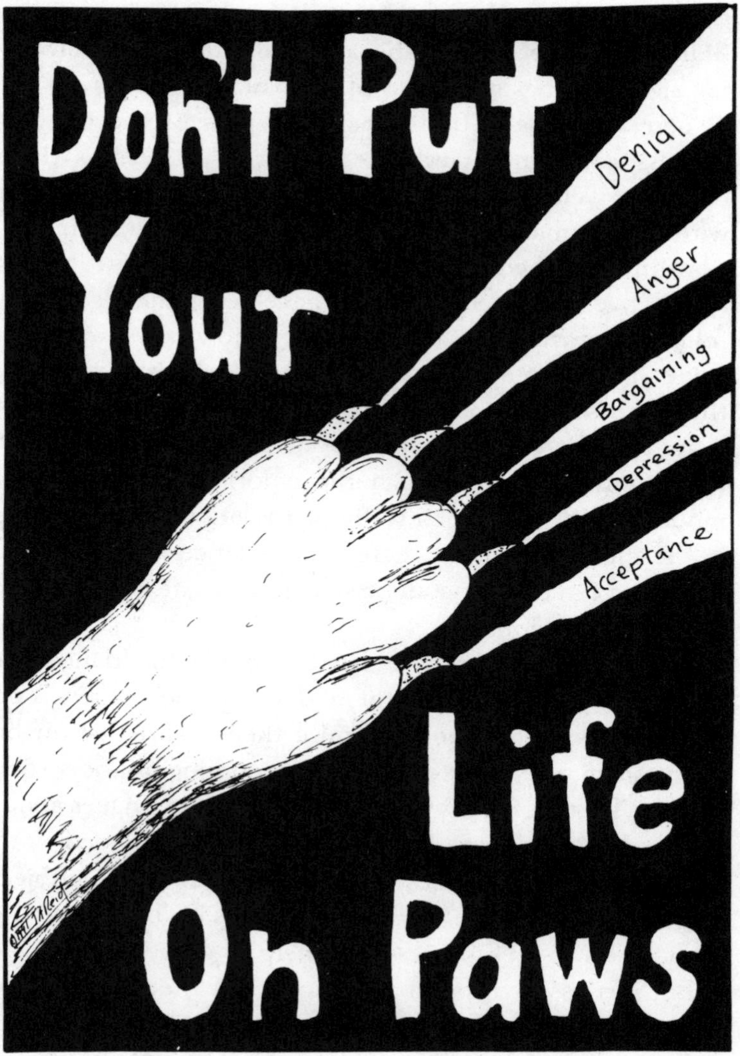

Don't Put Your

Denial

Anger

Bargaining

Depression

Acceptance

Life On Paws

portive support staff and a cat-free setting can overhaul a cat-dependent's twisted drives and realign their skewed values in an isolated pastoral setting. Some critics have complained that our admittedly harsh methods are at odds with constitutionally guaranteed freedoms. But, as the song has it, "Freedom's just another word for nothing left to lose." Isn't it better to sacrifice a sliver of freedom before there's nothing left at all?

Call our dispatcher at 1-900-976-CatD and we'll send a cat SWAT team out pronto. For a modest finder's fee you can have professionals intercede and have your friend, loved one, or casual acquaintance diverted to a soothing clinical hideaway. You may have seen the late-night TV commercials for our little spa. It's called Purrside. Our motto: "The healing begins when the squealing ends." We've found that the sooner you make the call, the better you'll feel—not just financially but physically as well. New studies are showing that "passive" cat-dependency can be just as devastating as its more active manifestations. You could be suffering from cat-dependency and not even know it!

To be sure, many of our "guests" are initially a little put off when they arrive at our little clinic. They often maintain (like truly sick individuals) that there is absolutely nothing wrong with them. But in a little while most of them wise up, er, warm up to the place. Here's an unsolicited testimonial from Betty, a current guest at Purrside: "At first I was a little steamed at my daughter for putting me in here, but it's been a revelation to learn how much family members can care. I'm hoping to return the favor as soon as I get out."

CHECK-IN CHECKLIST

As the phone company always says, sometimes all you need do to show you care is just pick up the phone. Usually, however, you also have to dial it. But in any case, you'll never know if someone you know needs Purrside—until you call. Take this quick quiz to see if we should reach out and put the touch on someone close to you. Check all applicable boxes.

- ☐ Do you know anyone who needs Purrside?
- ☐ Do you know their exact address?
- ☐ Do you know their Visa/Mastercard number?
- ☐ Hypothetically speaking, does 20 percent sound like a decent finder's fee?

Scoring: How Many Boxes Did You Check Off?

0 . . . . Poor. Don't call us, but we may call on you.
1 . . . . Good. Ring our 900 number for more information.
2 . . . . Great. Real operators are waiting to take your call.
3 . . . . Excellent. Call now for a free special premium.
4 . . . . Fantastic. Nice doing business with you.

Chapter Seven

WHAT'S IN? A NAME

Just scratch the surface and it hurts . . .
Imagine the pain that lies deeper.

—S. P. LUNKER

What's in a name? A cat by many other names is just as indiscreet. A cat's name, of course, most often says less about its temperament than it does about its master's. Cat's names fall into several general groups, and the recognition of these enduring types can give insight to friends and therapists alike. Each of these different categories offers clues to the exact nature of a cat-dependent person's sickness and the specific feelings of unworthiness that foster them.

Though this list is by no means all-inclusive and there is some overlap between types, most cat names fall roughly into these categories: Royalty, Exotic Foreign, Continental, Manly-Man, Ultra-Femme, and Cliché-Generic. In general, a cat's name is an unconscious expression of anxiety, a projection of the master's opposite that provides a pointer to his or her deep-seated insecurities.

Royalty has always been the most popular name category. Indeed, who hasn't been introduced to dozens of despotic pets sporting sobriquets such as Nefertiti, Napoleon, Josephine, Caesar, Claudius, and Cleopatra as well as mythological names from Athena to Zeus? These names essentially function as compensation for commonness. In today's bureaucratic-drone world, a touch of royalty has obvious appeal. Nobody names their cat "Visa Bill" or "Assistant Crew Chief" or "Return for Deposit"—all-too-actual reflections of modern mundane existence.

Exotic foreign names serve a similar escapist function. Especially popular among Americans, in line with their long-standing cultural inferiority complex, are continental names: Simone, Jean-Paul, Gunter, Victor-Emmanuel, Miguel, François, Nigel, and Ian are typical monikers. Middle Eastern, African, and Indian names are also coming into vogue such as Mohammed, Ashanti, and Ixtlan. Such names often serve as reminders of a much-savored vacation to foreign lands or a nostalgic desire for a halcyon "ethnic" past, often visited only through literature. Whatever the motivations, however, they all function as negations of the daily domestic mire.

Manly-man and ultra-femme names often mask deep-seated owner anxieties about sexuality and attractiveness. Any number of Brutuses, Maxes, and Harleys serve as cover for insecure men, nervous about their perceived virility. Similarly, for women unsure about their post-feminist position in a shifting world, femme names (Michelle, Anastasia, Chanel, Tiffany) offer a kind of sex-role mooring.

Some Even Later Signs of Cat Dependence

I'm not only the president of the hair-ball club for men--I'm also a client.

If one kitten makes me feel warm and wanted, then eight cats must be an absolute rush.

Conversely, those in a secure social and financial position are often eager to show their plebeian sympathies, their "down-to-earthness." Thus, just as Doreen's cat might be called Zsa Zsa, Zsa Zsa's might be called Doreen. Those who favor generic names like Puff, Little Kitty, or Mittens are either unbelievably simple or else unbelievably arch types likely to be performance-art poseurs or advertising-biz lampreys.

Yet after cataloging and recognizing these various types of insecurity and depravity, the battle is barely under way. Trying to convince cat owners that they are marked with these obvious telltale signs is likely to result in repeated salvoes of denial. In most cases, only when the cat-dependent person is in the final stages of breakdown is he or she likely to acknowledge the depth of agony and insecurity indicated by the seemingly casual naming process. But as the cat-dependency slogan says, "Just scratch the surface and it hurts. . . . Imagine the pain that lies deeper."

Friends and therapists can't really do much to change a person until they want to help themselves. Mental health is largely a self-service operation these days, especially in the initial phases. If a loved one is suffering from cat-dependence, try to be understanding, but not too understanding. You could easily lapse into the family dependence pattern of co-cat-dependence.

ACTIVITY

Pop Quiz

If you were going to choose a pet name for a creature known to gnaw the heads off songbirds and spend hours a day licking its genitals, what would it be?

- ☐ Genevieve
- ☐ Cleopatra
- ☐ Sabrina
- ☐ Anastasia
- ☐ Marilyn
- ☐ Annabelle
- ☐ Buford Pusser

Answer: None of the above—though Buford Pusser is closest to the true feline spirit. If you chose any of the others, chances are you're cat-dependent.

Chapter Eight

CO-CAT-DEPENDENCE AND "ADULT KITTENS"

The ties that bind strange bedfellows

—MARKY D. SAHD

Everybody's got one. A family, that is. And where there are families, there are family problems that need to be processed—not to mention family therapists who need their payroll checks processed. Yet things often have a way of working out for the best: families with family problems seek family counselling and the family counsellor gets his or her paycheck (which in turn keeps the family counsellor from having marital problems that would force him or her to go to family therapy, thereby avoiding quite a vicious circle of family problems). This of course doesn't solve the original problem that prompted the sessions, but it is progress nonetheless, and, as such, it is a positive sign.

Often, complicated as it might sound, things get worked through and things get worked out, yet they don't get worked throughout. That's because cat-dependency family issues are not only among the most ramified, they are also among the most complex. Part of this so-called "matrix of complexativity" stems from the sheer proliferation of relationships.

In many cases there is more than one family system functioning (or often, dysfunctioning), i.e., cats have kittens even as human parents have children. Birth-order traumas and cross-dependency relationships are frequent complications.

Research shows that middle children are especially prone to form attachments to cats. Yet first children, when they do fall prey to cat-dependence, fall harder—they do everything in a bigger way. But youngest children also have it tough, don't get me wrong. Standard birth-order analysis, however, leaves many questions up in the air. Why does an oldest child have the greatest difficulty with a middle kitten? Why do "baby" humans have such toxic relations with eldest cats? Are the children and spouses of cat-dependents doomed to their own nightmare of co-cat-dependency? What gives? But, more importantly, what takes?

CLAW AND ORDER

This whole constellation of issues has been broached in a rather abstruse way by Dr. Klaus Hooks in his book *Claw and Order: Adult Kittens of the Children of Cat-Dependent Co-Adults*. If you think cat-dependency is a slippery concept, give *Claw and Order* a wide berth. (Even most researchers find "Co-Adult" to be a problematic formulation, i.e., they "don't know what the hell it means.") Murky with statistics and choked with analysis, this tome is nonetheless a sort of Bible for the burgeoning "Adult Kitten" movement.

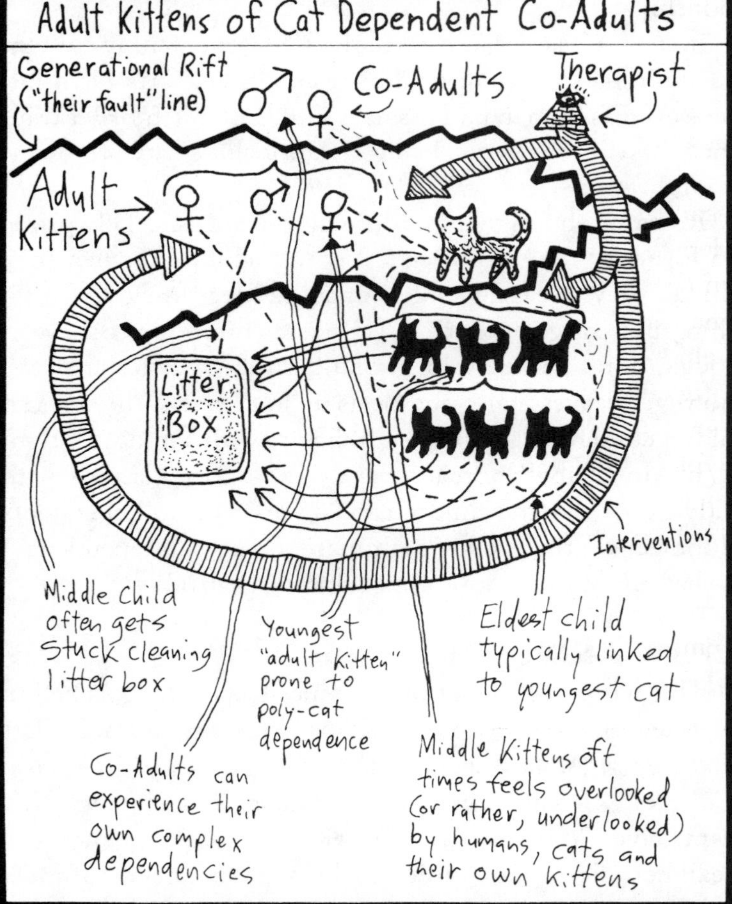
THERAPY ILLUSTRATED
Adult Kittens of Cat Dependent Co-Adults
Generational Rift
("their fault" line)
Co-Adults
Therapist
Adult Kittens
Litter Box
Interventions
Middle Child often gets stuck cleaning litter box
Youngest "adult kitten" prone to poly-cat dependence
Eldest child typically linked to youngest cat
Co-Adults can experience their own complex dependencies
Middle Kittens oft times feels overlooked (or rather, underlooked) by humans, cats and their own kittens

"Adult Kittens" are so called because humans raised in a cat-dependent home are said to adopt the feisty qualities of an immature cat, which initially may seem "cute as a dickens," but which ultimately proves self-destructive to the parasitic Adult Kitten and dangerous for the host "Co-Adult" as well. Conversely, cats in the same environment assume something of the dominant human role.

Adult Kittens maintain that they've been marred and scarred by childhood wrongs perversely nurtured in a cat-dependent environment. They feel that they can't move on in their adult lives until they reenact their childhood traumas in front of their entire family unit (or on public-access cable TV). Family therapy sessions with Adult Kittens are often frisky, as you might expect. But unlike harmless kitten games, in therapy, people can be hurt (indeed, in a typical therapeutic situation *everyone* is hurt to begin with—and there's nothing more dangerous than a wounded animal, especially the human animal).

Viewed through the long lens of an aggrieved life, small wrongs loom large. Remember, it's not how big your problems *are* that's important, it's how big they *feel*. And, as always, it's the therapist's job to read between the whines.

"I remember when I was six," Steve tells his mother with real anguish in his voice. "You took that dump truck from me and . . . and . . . and gave it to Billy. It was *my* truck. How *could* you? You always liked Billy better anyway. That time you took him for a ride in the car and left me home, I felt so abandoned."

Stevie's mother, hopelessly mired in denial, counters: "But Stevie, Billy needed stitches because you whacked him in the head with a hockey stick while he was sleeping. I had to drive him to the hospital.''

''See! You're always taking his side.''

It's just another day in the co-cat-dependent trenches. These family therapy sessions are chaos incarnate, involving various children and several generations of cats. The cats and kids sometimes get into hissy-fits, but it helps the therapist see how the humans take sides and interact. Scrape away the petty sibling rivalry in such situations and you'll eventually hear something like: ''You always liked Stevie's cat best.''

Now that's the voice of pain.

Once you get to that pain, you've got to process it. But before you get to that point there's usually a long stretch of what is known as ''interpersonal QRM,'' or, more simply put, static. (Adult Kittens have their own way of signifying this whole lotta nothing. Instead of saying, ''blah, blah, blah'' as many people do to signal conversational ballast, Adult Kittens like to say, ''meow-meow-meow.'')

Before getting to (and through) the real pain in therapy, you've got to get through the fake pain—which nonetheless feels like it hurts to the people experiencing it. Indeed it's a frustrated patient who finally gets in touch with his or her feelings only to find out that what he or she is feeling is not real pain, but psychological phantom pain. Needless to say, differentiating between real and fake pain can be a real pain for the therapist.

Chapter Nine

CAT-CHANNELING FOR CURRENT-LIFE REGRESSION

Those who forget the past are condemned.

—FAMOUS QUOTATION

You're probably familiar with the New Age concept of "trance-channeling" for past-life regression. This is a technique in which a person is hypnotized or otherwise entranced and led back past the birth barrier by a highly paid "channeler." Under such guidance, subjects experience previous incarnations in preternaturally vivid detail.

In such trance-channeling, people typically describe being members of ancient royal families, foot soldiers at famous battles, or relatives of Elvis. Skeptics of this "New Age sewage" sometimes wonder why so few people seem to have led mundane past lives, especially in contrast to subjects' invariably prosaic current existences. In an almost algebraic equation, the exotic nature of past lives seems curiously reciprocal to the tedium inherent in the subjects' contemporary incarnations. (See "Factorials of Fame, Infamy, and Anonymity'' in the *Journal of Psychological Fabulations* by Hailey N. Lockley.)

In contrast, my process, ''cat-channelling for current-life regression,'' is completely different, yet in many regards strikingly similar. No, this isn't the past lives of the pet wreaking havoc on the master. (That possibility has been explored in detail by New Age researchers—see especially, ''Cleopatra's Cat Wrecked My Marriage to a Holy Prostitute'' in the May issue of the *Wutme Reader*.) Instead, this is the condition whereby affection that should be directed toward our fellow humans is mischannelled.

In many middle-American homes the expression of love and affection between and among family members is suppressed, while the family pet becomes the emotional focus. People who can't openly express love for their parents or siblings or children can often be found lavishing attention on Fluffy (''Oh she's such a good good good good good little kitty-cat.'') In addition to the dangerous atrophy of vocabulary skills exhibited here, there are greater risks. The family pet, swollen with affection, can become a raging vortex of petulant frenzy or surly indifference. In this way, short-circuited energy powers the cat's rampant id even as it starves the people around us of their emotional nourishment.

BIG SLACK ATTACK

Furthermore, in a complex of behaviors not yet fully understood, this pattern leads some to emotional regression bordering on the infantile (of which vocabulary atrophy is just an early symptom). Because, as we have seen, cats don't just *get* extra slack for their ''independent''

New Age Cat

ways—they take it. And the people they take it from are the ones who may need it most. Many cat-dependent women, needless to say, don't find their boyfriend's erratic behavior as endearing as their cat's. (Imagine Cindy describing her man Mike like this: "He's just an animal sometimes, and he's so cute. Some nights when he doesn't come home I worry, but he can take care of himself. I'm just happy when he gets home in one piece." This, of course, is actually Cindy discussing her cat, Max.)

By diverting feelings that should go to humans and worshiping the cat's enslaved independence, the cat-dependent person lives a sham life—professing to admire the cat's manipulative aloofness and random mating behavior, when in fact he or she would run like hell from others who exhibited those traits. It's another sad case of looking for love in all the wrong places. Of course there are women who seek men that treat them as an alley cat would—but there are already dozens of self-help books out there for those gals. We're up to something different here.

THE INFLUENCE OF FRED

In order to carefully delineate the differences between the New Age notion of channeling and my more specialized construct, it is necessary to probe the New Age's amorphous foundations. Central to this mind-set are the conceptions of the influential Vienna-beef-heir-turned-vegetarian-visionary known simply as "Fred."

It was Fred who joked that, "Sometimes a Polish sausage is only a Polish sausage." He was also the first one to postulate that "all descriptions of reality are inadequate, particularly if you're trying to describe to the police the portion of reality that absconded with your color TV."

Fred also put forward the curious notion that evolution was only a temporary backwater in the universe's general flow of entropy. In other words, higher animals are only an eye-blink in creation *(augenblicktdieweltgegehen)*, their "purpose" being the excavation and rapid breakdown of complex coal and oil deposits into simpler, more inert forms. Thus evolution, in the Fredian scheme, while seeming to

Fred's Three Phases of New Age "Development"

GENIAL

Open-minded to the point of ventilation

If he thinks that ritual murder is the way to go, hey, that's his trip. You know, far be it from me, so to speak, you know what I'm saying. You have to walk a mile in the other guy's shoes before you throw the first stone.

produce increasingly complex life forms and social systems, ultimately serves to increase chaos and decrease complexity.

Although some of Fred's ideas negotiate the border between profound and outlandish, his influence is beyond dispute. Unfortunately, he died young in a tragic Gemeinschaft accident, so many of the contradictions inherent in his works may never be resolved. He nonetheless left a literally incredible legacy for us to sift through.

Particularly germane for our purposes is Fred's personality model of the three phases of New Age "development." He uses the term *development* advisedly, in keeping with the entropic pessimism that pervades his philosophy. The three phases of this nonprogression, known jointly as "the healing stasis," are the Aural Stage, the Banal Stage, and the Genial Stage.

In the Aural Stage, New Age converts become aware of previously unregistered perceptions and conceptions such as auras, ESP, and the hidden costs of Free Checking. In addition, they learn that their own past lives are more important than other people's current ones.

In the Banal Stage, New Agers discover the revelations of common knowledge and mundane metaphors (no two snowflakes are alike yet all cornflakes are . . . dull, soft coal becomes a glittering diamond under geological pressure whereas bright-eyed college students become squidly MBAs under economic pressures . . . if you're not part of the solution, you're part American).

In the Genial Stage, the final phase of Fred's healing stasis, the New Ager approaches a kind of intellectual democracy—all ideas being equally true. When individuals reach this pure level, known alternately as "microwave Nirvana" and "naptime," a New Age person becomes so open-minded that there's a draft up there—and we're not talking troop mobilization.

The preceding isn't intended as a universal condemnation of the crystal-gazing crowd and their navel-gazing forerunners. But the New Age mind-set is an increasingly prevalent underlayer for individuals with various dependency disorders. Though nobly intended as a path to spiritual growth, New Age systems often produce spongy individuals—human beings that have been described as "righteous pudding" by detractors. Unfortunately, these puddings are especially prone to predations by prowling cats.

Chapter Ten

THE MAN WHO MISTOOK HIS WIFE FOR A CAT

Imitation is the sincerest form.

—EDITED PROVERB

This case study is excerpted from the best-selling book by clinician and writer Olivoil Snaks. The good doctor specializes in breaking his patients out of the workaday gridlock of stupefaction and boredom that increasingly zombifies millions. Dr. Snaks has been successful with any number of hard cases and lost causes: couch potatoes, factory workers, sales clerks—even CPAs. In this groundbreaking case he liberates a couple who are suffering from a prototypical case of cat dependency, yet, incredibly, they don't even realize it!

As always, Dr. Snaks's theoretical jumping-off point is an insight gleaned from Maswell's Hierarchy of Nerds, i.e., all sentient creatures (and some junior high school students) go through predictable stages of mental development. Using cutting-edge chemical therapy, pop-culture iconographic analysis, and other experimental techniques, Dr.

Snaks tries to help push those who are stuck spinning their wheels in one stage to drive on to the next level.

On the surface, Bob and Katharine seemed typical for a couple who had been married for twelve years. Their life was routine and relatively uneventful. As in the early scenes of a Hollywood Western, things were quiet—*too* quiet. Beneath this placid veneer was a roiling tempest and an emotional volcano building toward a deadly eruption that could torch their relationship once and for all like the big blast and tidal wave at the end of that muddled action epic, *Krakatoa, East of Java.*

Bob and Katharine, on the face of things, were a lot like television's Ward and June Cleaver—Bob was the breadwinner and Katharine the homemaker. They couldn't have appeared more normal. Bob got up early five days a week, had some breakfast, read the paper, trained it to the office, navigated the swamp of office politics at a big corporation, and managed to wade home through it all at the end of each week with a decent paycheck.

Kitty (and what an ironic nickname that proved to be) got up early, cooked breakfast, went shopping, cleaned house, endured mind-numbing soap operas (on which failed singers imitating actors got paid to act as if they were singers), and munched bonbons all afternoon. Still, for all that, she had dinner ready every night when Bob slogged in. Yet something was wrong. Neither one of them felt as fulfilled as the husbands and wives they saw every night on TV.

Bob and Katharine, though superficially normal, were set off from the TV Cleavers, et al., by their uncharacteristic paucity of offspring. (In other words, what about the Beaver?) Their paternal instincts did have an outlet, however, in Penelope, their pet Tabby. Bob seemed to focus all of his loving attention on Penny, while his wife became more erratic and withdrawn and, to Bob at least, increasingly mysterious. I soon flashed on it—this "harmless" kitten was the key to solving the whole puzzle.

My first clue that all was not well was the way Bob addressed his wife by calling out, "Here Kitty, Kitty, Kitty." At first I dismissed this endearment as idiosyncrasy, if not plain idiocy, but it proved to be much more. Sometimes the simplest things can be paramount in shaking these ambulatory comatose cases out of their doldrums.

When our therapy session bogged down due to Bob and Katharine's general inertia and unwillingness to discuss their feelings (or much of anything else), I suggested that progress might be aided by the administration of a drug that had been effective with other such "loads," as recalcitrant patients are sometimes known. The drug is an experimental psychoactive organic compound developed in Mexico that is known by the chemical trade name "*El Dope*," though there are countless generic equivalents.

The drug helps to cut through the dull cocoon of the everyday, although you must be careful to prescribe the proper dosage or the drug produces its own characteristic lethargy. It's a calculated risk. I've found that it's often worth the gamble. It's necessary to temporarily arrest the symptoms and work back from the frozen situation in order to counter the psychological lockjaw that sets in. El Dope is a social lubricant that tends to loosen things up gradually. Because if I've learned anything, it is that the mummification of the mundane must be unraveled layer by layer. Do it all at once and the patients may not be able to cope with the shock. But each case has its own logic, and Bob and Katharine's problem ended up resolving itself on fast-forward.

As the drug worked its relaxing magic, I questioned the couple gently about their relationship—its genesis, subsequent development, and current moribund state. When I merely suggested that Bob seemed to express more feelings for Penelope than for Kitty, it all came pouring out.

They both quickly realized that Bob had reversed the flow of emotion in the household, diverting his energies from a loving wife to an indifferent cat. It was a complicated mass of overlapping feedback loops with the wires crossed in several places so that only Penelope was getting any power. As a result, wife and kitten flip-flopped—with the cat mellowing and the wife wigging out.

"Oh, wow," observed Bob, when he realized what had been going on.

Katharine, though less verbal, seemed similarly blown away by the whole scene. She suggested that they order a pizza. Bob said, "Great idea!"

But all great ideas take time. While we waited for the pizza we discussed relationships and I agreed to visit regularly to check their progress and refill their prescription. After what seemed like a long time we all realized that we couldn't just wait for the pizza—someone had to order it!

We all had a good laugh about that, but it was also a valuable reminder: if you want something good in life, *you* must make it happen.

Are you a feline junkie? Five tell-tale symptoms

Chapter Eleven

WOMEN WHO LOVE CATS TOO MUCH (and the Men Who Wind Up in the Doghouse)

And love won't hurt anymore.
—"LOVE BOAT" THEME

At the risk of being branded a repeat offender, I must admit that this chapter is a reprise, in miniature, of an earlier book of mine with the same title. This bonsai version of a book, if you will, is necessarily somewhat contorted by space limitations. But I like to think that this dwarf has its own twisted beauty. The full-size version, which you may nonetheless want to purchase, is chockful of checklists, white space, helpful hints, and comments from regular people such as yourself as well as hints that may be helpful to you. In addition, there is an inventory of activities and commentaries to aid in coping (what I refer to elsewhere as active cope-ativity).

I repeat here, not just to fill space and pad out *Cat Dependent No More: Learning to Live Cat-Free in a Cat-Filled World*. No, I think ecological prudence precludes that sort of irresponsible waste. Rather, this iteration is a recap stemming from the fact that my early insights paved the way for my subsequent formulation of cat-dependency as it is now in the process of being reprocessed here. And while I'm no longer focused on gender-specific analyses (as opposed to my current gender-general construct) there is much to be gleaned from my early study of the distaff half, even if I do have to say so myself.

"Women," I wrote in the aforementioned, aforewritten volume, "as the traditional emotional 'givers' in our society, have the most to lose when they encounter 'takers' as sociopathological as the common house cat. Indeed, in a curious negative feedback loop of guilt, women often feel that the more they give, the less they have actually given."

And then I wrote:

"Men, the traditional takers in such binary relations with women, may find that they are not 'bad' enough in the current competitive situation. The pitch has shifted under their feet. It's no longer a level playing field and, in any case, the cat has the home-field advantage. Moreover, when women adopt a masochistic game plan they tend to go for the gold. Why choose a man who may be a metaphorical tomcat when they can have the real thing?"

Why, indeed?

In order to answer this rhetorical question, I found it necessary to probe the pecularities of this antisocial dynamic. My research proved that in a love triangle with acute little cat, man is invariably obtuse (see diagram). In most such love triangles, the psycho-sexual conflicts remain latent. In other instances, however, they surface in peculiar ways.

Cat/Woman/Man Love Triangle

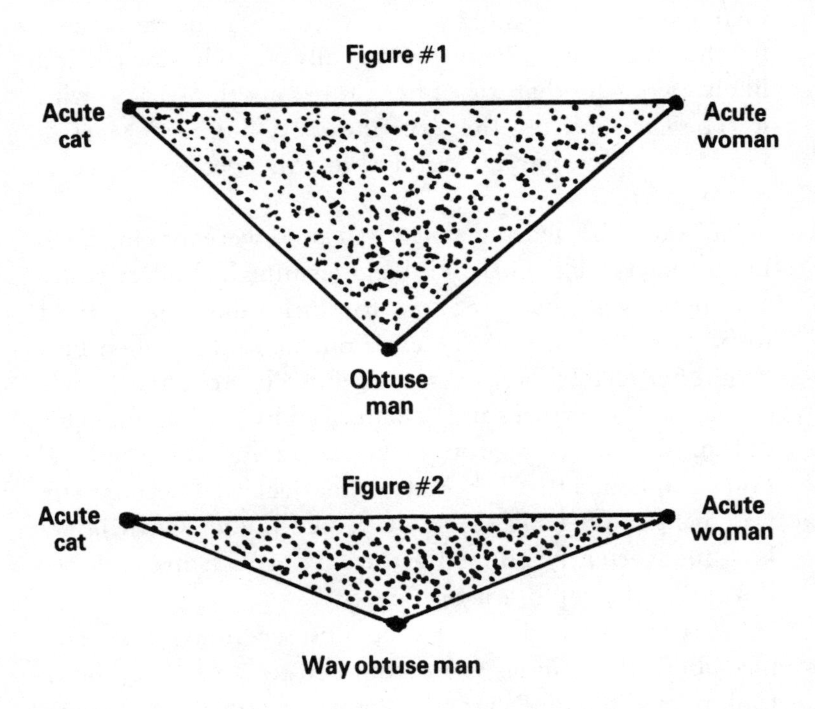

In a love triangle with acute woman and acute cat, man is invariably obtuse. The more man tries to push between them (fig. 2) the more obtuse he gets. This pressure makes cat and woman seem even more acute from the man's perspective.

Consider the case of Marry, an actress who specializes in playing headachy homemakers on TV. As she puts it, "A man may only be around for a few weeks. Your cat is there for the long haul." Marry is, ironically enough, single—and likely to remain that way if her cat has anything to do with it. The cat can't tell the story directly, but read Marry's version and see if you don't think the pet's message is getting across.

"The final break came when Phil and I were making love. Let me backtrack a little. Phil and Jasmine had never really gotten along all that famously, to put it mildly. Jazzy tried to be nice, I must say. She even put up with it when Phil taught her to fetch a hackey sack. But Phil rebuffed Jazzy's dinner-table overtures and got annoyed by her playful habit of leaping down from atop the bookcase onto his shoulder. Phil complained that I should get her declawed because she was mangling his silk suits. He yelped louder when Jazzykins inadvertently hooked a toenail through his earlobe. I'm *sure*. Like she did it on purpose.

"Anyway, after Phil overreacted by screaming like a maniac about that, things went from bed to worse [sic]. Jazzy took to stalking Phil's argyles—pouncing time and again at his ankles. But, as I was saying, the last straw was another fine kettle of fish. Though things had been rocky, Phil and I were keeping our relationship together somehow. Just between you and me and the tape recorder, our sex life was no problem—we had always been pretty great at doing the bone-dance. Until that last time, anyway. As we were making love, Jasmine was yowling like a cat in heat, which, ironically, she was. But Jasmine's singing, instead of hindering Phil's lovemaking, as it often did, seemed this time to increase the passion. And just as we got to the *moment*, Phil let out a howl to rival Jazzy's.

"It seems she'd clawed . . . I don't know how to put this but . . . you know, there's a part of the male body that looks a lot like a hackey sack. You can imagine. Phil was beside himself, and really not very understanding. It was his fault after all. But there was just no talking to him. You'd think he was the dumb animal in heat the way he carried on."

Of course, this is an extreme case. These conflicts are usually played out by proxy, with totem personal items standing in for the cat's despised rival. Tales abound of "special" sweaters that wind up shredded into common dust rags. Felines demonstrate an uncanny ability to search and destroy a man's favorite article of clothing (with the added bonus, for the cat, that it's also often the woman's least favorite article of the man's clothing, which has the effect of driving a wedge further between the man and woman).

In a similar vein, there are many recorded cases of a cat swallowing a shoelace from a man's prized sneaker. This lace chomping generally causes initial mystification/annoyance ("What could she have done with it?). But curiosity gives way to revulsion when, days later, the shoelace emerges from the other end of the cat. At the very least this causes consternation for man and woman, and potential constipation for the cat. In a worst-case scenario the pet dies (and given such an eventuality the relationship typically follows suit—in this way, the cat in effect comes back from the "other side" to destroy a relationship). At any rate, I concluded that everyone was a loser in such perverse love triangles and they all should seek professional help.

GRAPHIC VIOLENCE

We're probably all familiar with the Swedish interpersonal mapping system known as Sven Diagrams. But it wasn't until recently that a scientific breakthrough allowed a close-up look. Using psychic imaging technology developed at the University Havard Knox we can now clearly see that in the figure describing relationships that pass in the night, there is a feline catalyst speeding up the process.

The cat's history of destruction, however, is long and twisted, and not likely to be straightened out any time soon. I further noted, backgrounding my case studies with a nifty bit of cultural anthropology, how cat apologists of a mythical bent often emphasize that the cat was a sacred animal in ancient Egypt. It is well known, for instance, that the goddess Bast, responsible for fertility and a host of other deity duties, was always rendered in the guise of a cat. It was forbidden to harm cats in Egypt, although paradoxically thousands of them were mummified. The death of a cat was also said to have sparked a major war between the Egyptians and the Romans.

"But," I queried, "do we really want to follow the example of a society that mandated incest in its royal family and had servants killed so they could be sent into the next world mummified with their masters? Sure, the Egyptians built the pyramids, an engineering marvel that's never been adequately explained, but by all accounts they engineered this marvel with slave labor."

Sven Diagrams

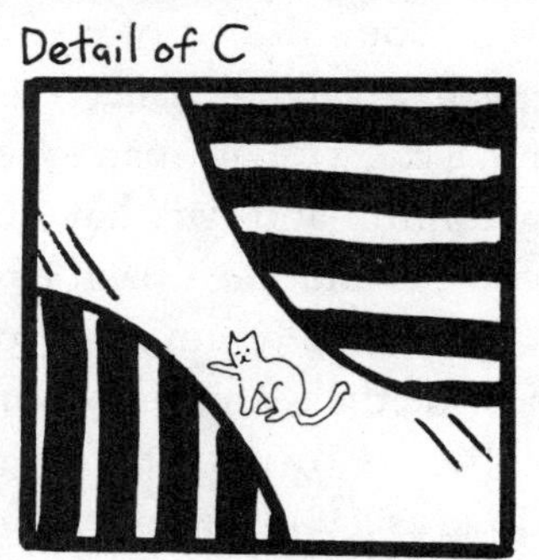

New psychic imaging technology provides a close-up view of how relationships often fail to connect due to intervention by a feline catalyst.

THE OLD MALE AND THE OLD MAILBAG

After the publication of *Women Who Love Cats Too Much*, I got a ton of mail—most of it favorable, which is nice. But some of the critical mail raised some good questions—as well as my own consciousness. Specifically, many readers wondered why I had neglected to cover love triangles involving two women and a cat. I hadn't entirely overlooked the question, but just assumed that any such triangle would be congruent to the one described, so you could draw your own diagram. And conclusions. (Indeed, one of my female researchers is now at work on an initial volume concerning this issue, tentatively titled *Feminism, Felines, and Fool-Tommery: Radical Lesbian Poetics of Color in Central New England, from 1857–59.*) Some of the least helpful remarks I received, however, came from women who were using their very real political oppression as a smokescreen for their very real personal problems, specifically cat-dependency.

Consider this self-styled "Ms-ive" from a member of the "Outrage Committee" of a Chicago activist organization.

"How like a lame male researcher to make the man a victim in a cat/woman/man love triangle. For your information, whimmin and kats have been enslaved by patriarchy for centuries and have been effectively disempowered as a result. Yet, despite ample opportunities for revenge and reprisals, neither whimmin nor kats vanquish man—he is ousted by his own petty competitive nature because he views love as a contest or a conquest but never the bliss of biological equals.

"In our collective we have no problems with rivalry between and among our cats or other sisters. The few minor lacerations, abrasions, and the occasional epidemic of cat-borne amoebic illness are a small price to pay to live in holistic harmony as we do. Your offering is obviously just one more tome that can only see women from the oppressive male viewpoint (or was that screwpoint?).

"It seems that it's just the cat's independent spirit that irks you. Anything that can't be bent to your male will is some kind of disease. And isn't disease merely a projection of male-dominated hard science into the realm of the bountiful female essence? You're obviously oblivious, but I'm sure there are some cunning linguists out there studying this problem who could explain it to you.

"It's time to bring the cat box out of the closet and move it right into the kitchen where we have it in our collective. Those who can't stand the savory smells of life are not living fully. I say, breathe deep the revelatory musk of feline and female. We decide who we are and where we go. In our freewheeling womanly way we sometimes refer to ourselves as "whymen," because we always have to ask ourselves that question. Clearly, there's no good answer to that one, and obviously you are too burdened by the oppressive yoke of patriarchy to understand us."

All I can say in response to this screed is that the sins of patriarchy aren't an alibi (or even an alibi-sexual) for self-destructive behaviors like cat-dependence. The astute among you will note the scattershot, or was that "cattershot," reasoning and the agile (if pointless and catlike) leaps in the argument. These, as we all know, are the hallmarks of advanced cat-dependence. Until these women realize that they are squatting in a rancid cat box of their own construction they will remain oppressed, and the yoke will be on them.

One other troubling line of criticism surfaced in the old mailbag after *Women Who Love Cats Too Much* was published. These were the letters from seemingly normal people who wrote in to say that while they realized that cat-dependency was a crisis for many, their cat had never caused them problems. At the time I didn't think too much of these letters, but later I remembered exactly how I had closed that volume.

"This book," I wrote, "is not intended as a criticism of 'responsible' cat owners. I have been assured that cats, when used in moderation, can be a relaxing diversion for some. Unfortunately, many can't 'just say no.' And it doesn't stop there, though many wish it could. It's hard to imagine how something so small, warm, and seemingly harmless can cause anguish for so many, but life is full of little mysteries, not the least of which are such poison puffballs."

If so many had missed such an obvious point, I had to wonder if the problem of cat-dependency was more widespread and insidious than I had previously imagined. Apparently, life with a cat produced synaptic disruptions both subtle and pronounced. One important aspect of these disruptions was the curious mirroring qualities of the illness—the cat-dependent eventually began thinking and even acting like a cat (this notion is in line with the commonsense observation that people ultimately come to look like their pets). Yet my support group knew about this mirroring aspect of cat-dependency before I had studied it clinically. They had an elegant slogan to sum up this inelegant behavior:

"Cat-dependency—it gives one paws."

Chapter Twelve

CATS AND POETS: THE OMINOUS PARALLELS

There's a fine line between assonance and asinine.

—NOGDEN GASH

The bond between cats and poets has often been remarked upon. Many poets claim the cat as a special muse—the not-quite-domesticated beast within. But what is the essence of this affinity? If poets are more in touch with their female side, as is often said, then the strong cat/poet bond makes sense within the gender-linked context of cat-dependency that we discussed in the previous chapter. The high degree of self-loathing poets traditionally exhibit is also consistent with the strong masochistic tendency among cat-dependents. Idealization, bordering on deification of the cat, is the most common manifestation of how this low self-esteem plays out—even among first-rate poets. Alas and alackaday, as they say.

Cats and Poets: The Ominous Parallels

Fig. 1: Pointless acrobatics in incredibly tight spaces

B "A burning leaf/A falling page./A new leaf... turning over in its grave."

Fig. 2: Coincidence?

A

B Kiddie Alliteration

"77,000 sibilant serpents hissed hysterically and slithered sheepishly across the sacred sassafras savannah."

And it doesn't stop there!

Cats and Poets, both:

- Are captivated by free food and drink
- Like to hear their own voices
- Never buy a new coat
- Have odd mating habits
- Don't pick up after themselves
- Get spooked at parties
- Scratch inappropriately
- Are extremely territorial
- Read the same amount of others' poetry.
- Earn the same

One feels the unseemly undertow of psychosexual longing as Shelley praises his cat in typically effusive style:

> O bard-like spirit! beautiful and swift!
> sweet lover of pale night;
> The dazzling glory of thy gold-tinged tail,
> Thy whisker-wavering lips!

Swinburne, too, heaped it on in a way, that, if not quite "dirty," appears not exactly clean either:

> All your wondrous wealth of hair,
> Dark and fair,
> Silken-shaggy, soft and bright
> As the clouds and beams of night,
> Pays my reverent hand's caress
> Back with friendlier gentleness.

Keats seemed to have a slightly less tenuous grip on reality than other poetic cat fanciers, as evidenced by this snippet from a sonnet:

> Cat! who pass'd thy grand climacteric,
> How many mice and rats hast in thy days
> destroy'd? How many tit-bits stolen?
> Gaze
> With those bright languid segments green,
> and prick
> Those velvet ears—but pr'ythee do not stick
> Thy latent talons in me . . .

The largest dent that the cat/poet connection has made in the popular consciousness is, of course, T. S. Eliot's whimsical *Old Possum's Book of Practical Cats* (which later mutated into the Broadway musical smash *Cats*).

US VERSES THEM

Less is known in general about the lesser poets who bask in deserved obscurity. But they too scribble frantically about their (all too) familiars. As I have crisscrossed the nation promoting the therapeutic concept of cat-dependency, I have encountered countless bargain-basement bards intent on convincing me of their cats' unique merits. They touch on the same themes and attitudes as the greats, but these verses go beyond mere poetics into gut-wrenching pathos. They range from the depths of doggerel to a blank-verse tabula rasa; from a heroic style that could only be called Walt Witless to something more like Edgar Allen Po' White Trash. One typical limerick, for example, begins, "There was a Burmese from Bangkok. . . ." Well, you get the idea.

Often this uneasy poesy focuses on the beloved's name, as in this ode to "Josephine":

There is a royal tease named
Josephine
the couch is her castle,
she's the queen
of all she surveys
though she sleeps all her days
under the steady gaze
of her subjects,
who love her dearly
de-flea her yearly

and understand her clearly
in unfathomed ways.

The deification and mythification shown here is fairly typical, as are the rudimentary verbal skills (which, we have seen previously, are characteristic of the cat-dependent). From the noblesse oblige of "Josephine" we pass to an entertainment star persona linked to an awkward ecological theme:

They call her Ertha Kitten
Cat-woman namesake
Earth mother to be
she means the world
the mean, mean old world
to me.

Clearly the withdrawal from life and the placing of the burden of ecological efficacy on the kitten is unrealistic to say the least. Some others process their passivity by going for social relevance and fashionable pessimism in a kind of dystopian beatnik mode:

Cat Find a Thrill
Indignant undercat
back-alley Zeus
dances across a stage
of stomped gray styro cups,
shattered glass and haunted stains.
Skipping toe-dance
thru Shards 'n' Things
the nu back-alley boutique.

Little Boutique come blow your own horn
the sheet's in the dumpster, the hobo's have corns,
the homeless forlorn, the hapless forewarned.
This different breed of cat
has his pick of the litter
and there's always plenty of that
for this indignant Other cat.

Some carry this relevance thing from the subpar to the ridiculous. A case in point is this self-styled "rap street knowledge" (which came complete with drum-machine instructions) from a young man who referred to himself only as "Vanilla Lice."

Y'all and the Pussycat

Y'all and the pussycat
went to see (and be seen)
in a superfly sequined coat.
They took all their posse
and plenty of money
and danced to the Big Blue Note.
Y'all looked up 2 the stars above
As they sampled a funky guitar.
O lovely Pussy,
O Pussy, my love
what a fly young Pussy U R,
U R, what a fly young
Pussy U R.

PROSODY AND CONS

But beyond all these amateurish odes to a cat is a darker parallel these poems can only illuminate obliquely or by indirection: the uncanny matching of poets' and cats' personality types. It seems that there is a subtle distinction between artistic temperament and feline distemper (and it may be a distinction without a *difference*, as the French like to say). Anyone who has seen poets bristle at the mention of their wordsmith rivals can't help but be reminded of a cat "getting its back up." Recovering cat-dependents instinctively feel this cat/poet affinity. Both cats and poets are often surly, oafish, indifferent, standoffish, iconoclastic, and erratic. And those are their good qualities. As one perspicacious cat-dependent put it, "If I wanted to associate with arrogant, self-obsessed loners, there are plenty of poets out there to fill the bill—what do I need with cats?"

Another cat-dependent echoed these sentiments:

"If I wanted to associate with arrogant, self-obsessed loners, there are plenty of poets out there to fill the bill—what do I need with cats?"

And yet another concurred:

"What he said. Boy, that's *it*. Couldn't have put it better myself. No siree. Friggin' cats. Lame-ass poets. Why do I need the aggravation?"

Alas, nobody needs the aggravation. But we *owe* it to our fellow humans, however prosaic, to make an effort. Granted, endless assonance and rampant alliteration can be just as asinine as scattered litter all over, but with patience, even poets can learn civility. Sadly, the same cannot always be said for felines.

Chapter Thirteen

SERIAL CAT-DEPENDENCY: ONE DAMNED THING AFTER ANOTHER

Forgive and forget? Forget it!

—ANNE NONIMUS

As a recovering cat-dependent you must be constantly on guard. No sooner have you "put out the cat" and begun to block the memories, than other cat-addicts (not nearly as recovered as you) are ready, willing, and able to resupply you with a "cute little kitten."

They wouldn't give booze to a drunk or heroin to a drug addict, but people are still insufficiently aware of the dangers of cat-dependence. Even if consciousness of cat-dependence as a dangerous addiction were greater, however, there would probably always be plenty of people willing to share their misery. Whenever people offer me kittens, I give them a copy of the pamphlet, *Why Fluffy Can't Breed: Calling a Spayed a Spayed*. That usually quells the "giving" impulse. The pamphlet lists facts and figures about the

Illustration from the pamphlet, "Why Fluffy Can't Breed."

feline population explosion and the cost of raising the average pampered American cat (the same as the cost of raising a Third World child).

The focus of the pamphlet is the economic cost, but greater still is the psychic and spiritual toll. This, however, is much more difficult to explain. In addition, people sometimes react violently to the news that Mittens is a menace to many of us. And so, these pussy pushers act like there's nothing wrong with dealing in this dangerous uncontrolled substance. There is little stigma attached to this kind of pushing, because no profit or other obvious advantage is gained, yet it can be as devastating as dispensing narcotics.

Don't get me wrong, now, there is nothing "wrong" with recreational use of cats in our society—if you can handle them. But some of us, when we handle them, can't handle them, if you get my meaning.

BORN TO BE MILD

Many people have started noticing that the mild emotional "high" they get from cats is having a detrimental effect on their lives, even if they don't have a particularly wild pet. They tend to interact less with their fellow humans and therefore show less warmth and compassion for them. So, just as many people are saying "no" to drugs, so too are they saying "no" to cats. Different strokes for different folks, as they say, to each his own, and one man's meat is another man's poison. You go your way and I'll go mine. Isn't that what they say?

That being said, many people nonetheless go through life jumping from one cat to the next with all their excess emotional baggage in tow. These serial cat-dependents, the most typical manifestation of the syndrome, live their lives "one cat at a time" in a curious kind of moderation that masks the potentially harmful side effects of cat-dependency. Although some people own cats for decades with no visible side effects, eventually, most people come to some sort of crisis. They are human time bombs tick-tick-ticking away. Consider this note from a seemingly harmless specimen who wrote to me when I was filling in for a newspaper advice columnist:

> Dear "Dr." Reid,
>
> I know this is going to seem like the same sad old refrain to you, but I just keep singing it. Every time I'm doing well, coping with my life, I start recycling (or is it relapsing—I'm so befuddled I can't even distinguish between the two). No sooner do I get rid of one cat than someone gives me another. I mean, the grieving process for Mandrake isn't even through denial and already here comes a kitten called Katharine to steal my heart (and later rip it to shreds). All the unprocessed grief is just piling up like so much dirty laundry. The longer I wait to do anything about it, the more paralyzed I feel by it. It really stinks (the situation I mean, that bit about the laundry was just a simile). And then—just when I'm feeling like I'm finding a grip, getting a clue, taking control, assuming command—there's another cat, and then another, and yet another, and yet even still yet another. I know they call it "serial cat-dependency," but isn't there anything to be done for people like me? I've been through this so many times that it seems like co-redundancy.
>
> Getting Too Hairy

I told "Getting" that as serious as her situation was, she would be well advised not to be so glib about the devastating problem of "co-redundancy." Her obviously difficult situation warrants empathy, that's for sure, but think of those poor co-redundants out there who don't even have a problem to call their own; instead, they must share with others. Their splintered self-hood is denied even the perverse satisfaction of owning their own illness. Not only are there no best-sellers written about their problem, I have yet to hear of any in the pipeline. My heart goes out to them. Although cat-dependency is often given short shrift in the self-help world, co-redundancy has not yet amassed even a modicum of shrift.

That being said (and quite nicely, I must say), Getting's serial cat-dependency does indeed seem chronic. Perhaps she has taken that fateful step from re-cycling to re-psycho-ing—going from a mere mental lapse to a demented and diseased need for constant crazy-cat contact. Needless to say, she should consider seeking professional help. No, I'll go even further, she shouldn't just seek professional help, she should *find* it.

And yet, some are even further out on the ledge of their own personal problems. If Getting seemed "a couple sandwiches short of a picnic" (to quote Jung), some people are yet more obscured by a self-imposed delusionary haze of hubris.

Dear "Dr." Reid,

I am at the end of my rope, my wit's end, and am coming unglued. My cat Sabrina yowls every night as if in a menstrual fever even though she has been "fixed."

Whenever the morning paper comes, she pulls it apart and urinates on the Arts section—which is, incidentally, the only part of the paper I really like to read. The cat box is reminiscent of Hurricane Hugo's aftermath.

I feel that I probably should seek professional help. I'm ashamed, yet I know that what I'm feeling is totally natural and nothing to be ashamed of. If only I could self-validate, center myself, get in touch with my real feelings, learn to let myself go, and realize that I'm the only self I've got, I would be doing fine. Lord knows I haven't any real problems; I just feel all alone sometimes in the existential sense.

Alice Tribec
Television City, CA

I told Alice that I was going to have to penalize her for phrasing her question in the form of an answer, and left it at that. After my response was published, I felt a pang of remorse for being so harsh. But when I thought about it, I realized that it wasn't callousness on my part, but "tough love." It was just a wake-up call for someone who thinks that they can administer their own therapy. Freud could barely do it, yet *they* say, "Hey, no sweat." The sooner cat-dependents seek help, of course, the better it will be for them. Because sometimes, there's nothing sicker than thinking you're well.

Recovery from cat-dependence is a process. It's a process of being and of *being processed*, which takes time because progress is a process as well as a progression. It's a confusing process, I know, but that's progress.

Which isn't to say that it doesn't hurt and that there

aren't incidents of backsliding or "recycling." In other words, which *is* to say that it does hurt and there are incidents of backsliding or "recycling." As one of my patients said, "It's a cumulative hurt, deeper than any claw marks. Long after the stitches have healed and the new furniture has been bought, there is a psychological emptiness."

Psychologists call this psychological emptiness a "void," or a "dead spot," or more technically a "nether region of interpersonal space bounded by 'nothing' on all sides and 'not much more' in the middle." But whatever they call it, it is always tempting to try to fill it with another cat. That's why there's no cure for the disease of cat-dependence, just a lifetime of treatment.

Chapter Fourteen

HOOKED ON A FEELING: POLY-CAT-DEPENDENCE

Repeat and fade.

—POPULAR REFRAIN

If "monogamous" serial cat-dependents are ticking time bombs, their "polygamous" counterparts have already blown it. For them, a runaway chain reaction of cats has kicked in, obliterating any semblance of a normal life. They've fallen into a psychological pattern that dooms so many addicts: if one cat feels good, then ten must feel great.

Sylvia, a recovering hardcore cat-dependent, describes her initiation into the nightmare world of poly-cat-dependency.

"The first one's usually free," she says, "just to get you hooked. There's always somebody around offering to turn you on to some primo Tabby Red or a smooth British Blue. They feel so good that you never want it to stop. It starts with a kitten. Then another. And another . . . The next thing you know, you're a curiosity clip on the weekend news: 'An eccentric old woman died yesterday in a Northside bungalow. She is survived by two hundred cats.' Finally, I realized I didn't want to go out like that." Luckily, Sylvia sought help in time.

Julie, another recovering poly-cat abuser, also notes the difficulties of coping with increased feline tolerance.

"At first the warm rush of affection is really intense, but after a while it starts to fade. It seems only natural to try to recapture that feeling with another cat. It works for a while, then that feeling also passes. Pretty soon, of course, come the kittens, which is an entirely different rush. If you're not careful—and trust me, you're not—you get in over your head."

Hardcore addicts often spend much of their day "maintaining" their habit: "scoring" cat chow, brushing pesky long hairs (a.k.a. mane lining), sorting out feline "domestics" (and the ensuing trips to the vet), midwifing kittens, etc. Often these human "caretakers" spend so much time caring for their cats that they forget to care for themselves—particularly in the area of personal hygiene. The harbinger of this process is the inability, on the part of the cat-dependent, to smell trouble brewing, specifically the cat box.

Researchers—that is, those who search again—have hypothesized that this "olfactory assault prepares the psychological battleground for worse smells to come." In other words, "shit happens (to stink) but the anesthetized cat-dependent doesn't know." There may also be a psychological denial mechanism at work here. "He who smelt it, dealt it," as Bertrand Russell once said, inferring an all-too-human tendency to cover up and blame others.

The only way to escape this kind of extreme cat-dependency is to get a decisive grip and change your life once and for all through an act of ironclad personal will. Then you join a support group to make sure you don't change your mind.

If the road to hell is paved with good intentions, then the road to recovery from cat-dependence is littered with well-meaning addicts who have fallen by the wayside. The support group is there to give you a lift when you need it. (For a more explicit road map to recovery see Chapter 6.)

GETTING DOWN TO THE KITTY NITTY-GRITTY

Consider this cry for help from Sarah, a recovering poly-cat-dependent. "On my way over here," she told her support group, "I walked past the pet store just to test my strength [groans from the group] and I felt like I was doing fine. There was a squirming basket of kittens and they were all imploring me with their eyes, but I held strong [calls of 'Right on!' from the group]. But there was one sickly kitten off to the side, oblivious, overlooked. In some mysterious way, she reminded me of myself. She seemed so sad. I went inside just to touch her to see if she was okay. . . . Well, I just had to hold her."

With that, Sarah reached into her handbag and fished out the mewling kitten. The group burst into an uproar. After a yowling brouhaha, followed by a major scene and a total tsimmis, they convinced Sarah to return the kitten. But it wasn't easy. Never is.

Says Ludmilla, another poly-cat-dependent who's been there, "People always offer helpful advice such as 'Just say no,' but it isn't that easy. They don't know what it's like.

They don't know how it feels. They don't know what it feels like.

"Even though I'm strongly allergic to cats, every time I see a kitty calendar or the Sunday comics, I feel this incredible *need.* I guess that never goes away, but I hope it gets a little easier eventually. I try. I try. Sometimes, in some cozy den, when another cat-dependent offers me a little purr-bag, I say, 'No thanks, I'm trying to cut down.' It's my effort to get the point across subtly that cat-dependency is just another bad habit. But it's not something other users really want to hear. And until they want to hear it, there's not much I can do—except maybe turn up the volume a little."

But "turning up the volume" on others isn't feasible for cat-dependents until they decrease the volume of cats in their own lives to zero.

Chapter Fifteen

BOUNDARY ISSUES: BOUND TO LOSE

I think I am, therefore, am I?

—RENE DECAT

One area where cat-dependents are bound to have problems is boundary issues. The cat-dependent's chronically trampled self, sometimes known as the "stupor ego," ensures a depressed perspective on the situation. And, as farfetched as it seems, cat-dependents begin to lose touch with where they leave off and where the cat begins. The cat-dependent may find it difficult to define the difference between their cat's feelings and their own. Needless to say, the cat isn't slain by such ambivalence. But for the master, it's a gray area that tends to expand—until the cat-dependent is completely in the dark. A failure to post proper boundaries, in effect, leaves the cat-dependent person psychologically bound and gagged.

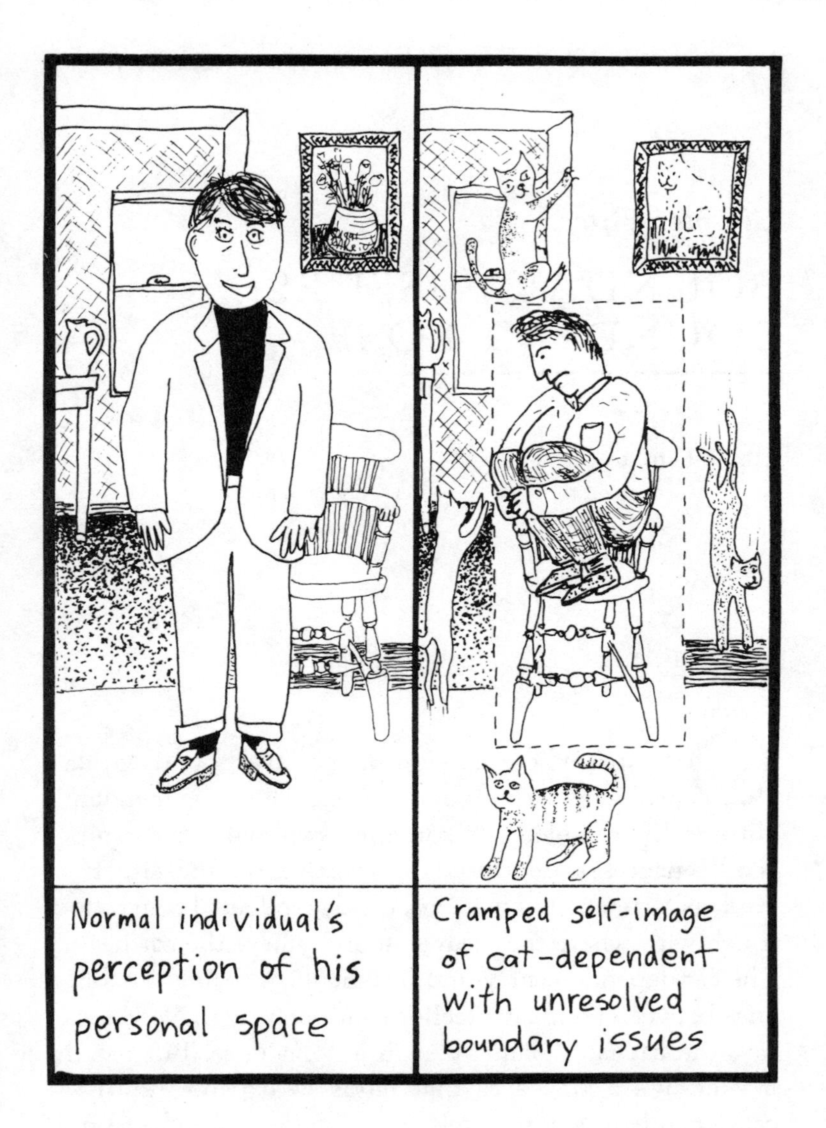
Normal individual's perception of his personal space
Cramped self-image of cat-dependent with unresolved boundary issues

You set boundaries because:

- ☐ You have to know where you stand
- ☐ You have to know where you *don't*
- ☐ It's hard to tell where "you" leave off
- ☐ It's hard to tell where the "other" begins
- ☐ It's hard to tell where you get off (or how)
- ☐ Without borders, you will be bordering on insanity
- ☐ They tell you where to stop
- ☐ They tell people where they can go

Cat-dependents feel unaccountably responsible, as we have seen, for their cat's destructive behavior. They take the weight of the burden of the onus onto (and unto) themselves. Their cats are their various crosses to bear as they sacrifice everything else and then some.

- ☐ Jennipher is sorry she didn't call back, but Rhodan bit through the phone cord because he's been neglected lately.
- ☐ Steven can't go out Friday because he's got to scrub the cat box and environs for the third time this week.
- ☐ Sharon worries that the hair dryer is terrifying her cat Tiffany—so she's late to work again.

The human ability to rationalize is obviously as genetically ingrained as the cat's gymnastic antics. But while cats are known to always land on their feet, the same, sadly, cannot be said for humans. Most cats could easily survive a fall from three stories, while, as we have seen, many people can't even cope with their own life's story.

After months or years of Tabby terrorism or Siamese sorties into their personal space, the addled addict can be forgiven for not knowing which way is up or where to draw the line. Be that as it may, cat-dependents must somehow draw a line in the sand (though drawing one in the cat box is not recommended). As all cat owners know, these border skirmishes can be violent and may lead to full-blown war. Most frequently, however, what develops is a war of attrition that is more psychologically devastating than physically dangerous in any direct way. Yet the stakes are high: control of the self.

Once cat-dependents realize the battle they're in, they may justly demand reparations. Of course this situation is complicated by the fact that this border issue is also a boarder issue: cats rely on the terrorized cat-dependent for life's necessities. Although it may seem harsh, most military strategists recommend cutting the supply lines in cases like this. You may have to starve them out. Nobody said it was going to be easy. Once cat-dependents start recovering they become aware that they have been occupied (or at least pre-occupied) and begin gradually to reclaim their personal territory. Recovery sometimes just means recovering, in a very literal sense, the use of your apartment. And it is often a room-to-room battle. Armchair dominance struggles sometimes go months without resolution (indeed "sofa squatting" often continues indefinitely when the master's away). The only final solution to this problem, of course, is feline exile to the Humane Society, a step many cat owners aren't ready to take. The alternative is living a partitioned life—a conflict resolution strategy that hasn't proved too successful on the geopolitical level.

Another way to look at these boundary issues is to see personal boundaries as analogous to the margins on a typed page. The self is the typescript that conveys thoughts and feelings. The oblivion of catdependency is represented by the emptiness that frames the page. As the meaningless white space progressively impinges from the margins, less and less can actually be said. In other words, the slate of self-hood shrinks. As this happens, the tendency naturally arises to write simpler messages and to write them LARGER—in order to get *something* across.

This in turn only makes

matters worse because less can be said and the marginal "other" subsequently pushes in even further. Ultimately, in the worst-case scenario, nothing can be communicated at all. The "self" is totally blocked and the individual draws a complete blank.

Complete blank*

*Artist's conception

Chapter Sixteen

LET'S GET PHYSICAL; LET'S GET FISCAL

They give me cat-scratch fever
—TED "THE NOOGE" NUGENT

Although the focus of this book is largely psychological, our holistic approach to cat-dependence requires that we get physical as well as metaphysical. (At that point, we will be getting fiscal as well, but that's another issue.) When it comes to cat-dependence, the spirit may be willing, but if the body is unable, go fish. Sometimes, to quote that well-known maxim of probate lawyers, where there's a will, there's a wait.

Cat-dependency's physical aspect runs along a continuum of damage that doesn't stop at petty lacerations. The maladies range from rabies to ringworm and from cat-scratch fever to toxoplasmosis—the last being the most dangerous. Toxoplasmosis is a feline amoeba illness borne by cat feces. The cats are often symptomless (wouldn't you just know) while pregnant women who clean the cat box run the greatest risk of contracting the illness. The amoeba is present in subtoxic levels in a significant minority of cat owners. But what makes the infestation go "over the top" and affect some people rather than others is not known. Consult your local physician. Medical authorities can give a better description of this sometimes fatal detraction.

Yet transmittable diseases are a minor part of the physical damage of cat-dependence (unless you happen to be the unlucky fatality). More often, the physical ill effects of cat-dependence are indirect. Those little hurts add up, or, as we say, "have a cumulative effect." Let's see how this problem gets worked out.

Most cat owners know "instinctively" that there are certain times and places when and where their cats should not be hassled. But is this really instinct? Common sense and clinical studies show clearly that the cat owner's deference is most often a product of a pattern of abuse, physical and mental. Girl meets cat, cat scratches girl, girl gives cat "space."

SCENE AND HERD

Part of this general human acquiescence to the violence of cats stems from the fact that, genetically and historically, humans are social creatures while cats are solitary hunters. Humans, as herd animals, tend to "let someone else steer." (In other words, it comes down to, "Steer or *be* steer.") Cats, needless to say, are happy to drive you wherever they want to go.

In one study, cat owners and their pets were sealed in one-room apartments without air conditioning on Manhattan's Lower East Side and observed via videotape for several weeks in July and August. Researchers report that the humans reportedly grew "irritable," while the cats showed no ill effects.

In addition, the cats found ways to amuse themselves, often at the expense of their cellmates, while the humans' activities were limited to irate comments about real-estate speculation and rhetorical meteorological queries on the order of "Is it hot enough for ya, or what?" Watching the tapes, you can almost feel the humans' nearly palpable disempowerment, evident in their fatalistic choice of small talk. As the old saying goes, "Everybody talks about real estate, but nobody does anything about it."

But how did this powerlessness evolve? (A side issue, studied in tandem, was the emerging concept of "ness-ness," that is, the tendency to add suffixes to words in lieu of actually doing research—for a full treatment of this trenchant topic, consult Arty Kunst's important monograph, *Nessitivity: The Suffix Glut.*)

By examining the tapes of these experimental apartment sessions, researchers found that cats used a hit-and-run technique to stake out their territory. Feline tactics proved strikingly similar to those that have been successful in this century's guerrilla wars. Cats, it seems, never had to learn "the lesson of Vietnam," because they knew it all along. Indeed, there is some evidence that the Vietnamese may have learned a thing or two about guerrilla warfare from the intermittent sorties of the domesticated Siamese and Burmese cats that have long populated Indochina.

And if the apartment dwellers in this study were faced with the turf battles and tactics reminiscent of Indochina's ambush-prone wars, they were also often caught off guard by the hidden costs of this low-level conflict. Guerrilla

warfare invariably entails escalating psychological and economic costs. In strictest economic terms, as we have mentioned before, an American cat consumes more resources annually than the average person in the world's poorest nations. As bad as that might sound, the reality is even worse because cats aren't people, despite misguided cat owners' protests to the contrary. In fact cats, it can be argued, often make the leap from pets to pest.

And although it's an odious analogy for the cat fancier to accept, some researchers have determined the cat to be an urban apartment pest that ranks below the cockroach when judged by a number of objective criteria.

URBAN PESTS SQUARE OFF

	Cat	*Cockroach*
Number of diseases transmittable to humans	57	0
Percentage of population allergic to	17	0
Annual food expenditures for	$250	0
Annual medical expenditures (pest)	$195	0
Annual medical expenditure (human)	$65	0
Can you get them to poop where you like?	No	No
Can you keep them out of the garbage?	No	No
Can you keep them off the walls at night?	No	No
Likelihood they'll walk on the table while you're eating	1 in 4	1 in 100

Obviously, this study overlooks the "cuddly factor," where the cat comes out way ahead. And on the face of it, the cat gets the sympathy of even the most wretched cat-dependent. But also on the face of the cat-dependent there are scars, and they are, by definition, only on the surface. What lies deeper is an abyss more profound than anything merely physical or even fiscal. The real reason to get the kitten off your back is "you." If you don't think that's a good enough reason, you've got to keep reading.

Chapter Seventeen

COCOA-DEPENDENCE AND THE FUDGE FACTOR

The problem with all-consuming passion is
that it constantly eats away at you.
—FROM *The Boy Who Noshed Too Much*

Perhaps one of the worst things about dependencies is that they run in streaks. No sooner is one habit kicked than another kicks in. Call it a concatenation, a chain reaction that can enslave the unwary. It's a kind of emotional bondage, if you will (a kind of prison of feelings, if you won't).

I know a bit about these chains of love, because often the cat-dependents who come to me for therapy have first been dependent on any number of other persons, substances, behavior patterns, feelings, things, expectations—what have you (and increasingly, what have you not).

These dependencies are legion. For instance, a Roman Catholic researcher has pinpointed one rampant, debilitating syndrome known as "Mo'-Dependents," which induces financial and psychological hardships for millions worldwide. There is also an opposite syndrome—in which a potential tax loophole becomes a noose—known as "No-Dependents." And of course, over on the wrong side of the tracks, those addicted to prostitutes have been described by numerous researchers as "Ho'-Dependents."

In addition, there are the "Auto-Dependents." No, "auto" doesn't refer here to the automobile (though that dependence syndrome also has its well-documented negative side effects). "Auto" in this case means "self" and it's one of the nastiest disabilities yet studied. Nothing is more negatively self-centered than a person dependent on his or her self. If people who need people are the luckiest people in the world, then auto-dependents are their unlucky antithesis.

The list of dependencies could go on and on, but sometimes we must give in to "demon linearity" and get to the point. Nothing is lost in this case by taking the direct route, because, oddly enough, all roads in this maze of madness lead to cat-dependence. Viewed in one way, cat-dependence is the apex of the pyramid of dependency. Viewed another way it is the low point of an emotional landfill. In either case, it is the end of the line—all things lead up to it, or all things lead down to it. Paradoxically, it seems that "up" and "down" mean the same thing in the universe of dependencies. Dependent personalities, it is often said, don't know up from down, and now we can begin to see why.

COCOA-DEPENDENCE: THE BITTERSWEET SYNDROME

But if cat-dependence is the ultimate syndrome, there has to be a penultimate. Most often this second-to-last stutter step is cocoa-dependence. Succinctly put, it's a sweet tooth gone sour. Tragically, many people battle cocoa-dependence gamely only to lose a subsequent skirmish with cat-dependence. They discover that the emotional void left by kicking chocolate addiction provides a perfect opening for an opportunistic cat infection.

Like cat-dependence, cocoa-dependence is a largely female malady (and in this case, the larger the female, the larger the malady). But this female trouble is bigger than just the expanding waistline it often produces. Cocoa-dependents exhibit the same array of symptoms as those afflicted with other dependence syndromes. These include (but are not limited to):

- □ Neurotic compulsive behavior
- □ Self-destructive denial
- □ Various misery-loves-company mechanisms
- □ Blaming others
- □ Blaming "others"
- □ Increased "substance" tolerance and a commensurate increase in usage
- □ Inability to lunch without wine
- □ Inability to lunch without whining

But cocoa-dependence is not just a compulsive disorder, it's also a physical addiction. In a cruel trick of nature, the molecular structure of chocolate closely mimics that of a chemical in the pleasure center of a woman's brain. And due to the specific nature of this chemical, cocoa-dependence is closely bound to sexual addiction. The brain chemical that chocolate resembles on a molecular level is the one a woman's brain releases during orgasm.

This helps explain some of the passion women express

Are You Cocoa-Dependent?

for chocolate from an early age—but especially after puberty (it also helps explain men's relative immunity to cocoa-dependence). Sadly, most chocolate addicts acquire the habit "in the home," where it is subsequently spurred on by biological imperatives.

"When I was a little girl," says Chevonne, a recovering cocoa-dependent, "my mama used to give me little pieces of chocolate, so I always had 'the taste.' But it wasn't until I became a woman that my needs got really intense. And at 'that time of the month' I had to have just two things: pain pills and chocolates."

Yet despite the sexual/hormonal link, cocoa-dependence progresses along lines parallel to those of other dependencies. The situation is exacerbated by the fact that chocolate products are readily available "over the counter" and are erroneously believed to be harmless (with the only generally acknowledged side effect being obesity in extreme cases). As a result, uncounted innocents are steered down the dark corridor of chocolate addiction. Consider the case of Paula:

"For me," says Paula, "it started with chocolate chip cookies, then chocolate chunk, then chunks of chocolate. Before too long I began gravitating toward bars. At first I preferred the upscale Euro-trash imports, but then I found that "bulking" domestic brands was cheaper and provided a similar kick. For a while I even went generic, but that stuff is cut with strange additives that produce ghastly withdrawal symptoms."

While some have questioned whether cocoa-dependents suffer actual withdrawal symptoms or just something similar, the intense rush and subsequent emotional crash are reminiscent of cocaine psychosis and can induce depression (although once again no one has yet determined if this is bona fide depression or just something that mimics the symptoms). As with other addictions, cocoa-dependence is not merely physical—a whole dynamic social context impacts the individual and in turn gets impacted socially, resulting in an ongoing social-dynamic contextualization of impaction.

FOOD FOR THE THOUGHTLESS

This point is echoed by Joanie, a recovering cocoa-dependent sociologist (she's recovering from cocoa dependence—there is, as you might imagine, no known recovery program for sociology). "Food is an essential part of female socialization. Traditional gender roles center women within the universe of food: both in preparation and consumption. Just consider, if you will, for instance, to take just one of many examples, that the all-time most popular video game for women was Pac Man. The entire game is played in an oral mode: eat or be eaten (and if everything is properly prepared you can even devour those who would devour you).

"From an early age young females are encouraged to play gender-ghettoized cooking games and aid their role models in daily food preparation. They join in rigid social clubs that reinforce culturally dictated behavior templates that in effect force them to wear uniforms, and even act uniform. It's not surprising when they end up living uniform lives. For example, young girls often join the Brownies, where they are asked to behave like young ladies and always bring snacks to their meetings, which, not incidentally and even somewhat ironically, are, often, brownies. Given these overlapping matrices of influence, it's easy to see why food disorders, including cocoa-dependence, are endemic for females."

Joanie certainly said more than a mouthful, but she's definitely on to something.

Yet it's a classic common sense case of nature versus nurture, chicken or the egg, holism or reductionism, six of one, half a dozen of the other, one man's meat is another man's poison. Given her background in sociology it's understandable that Joanie leans toward the nurture side of the equation. And it does seem the more dominant aspect in this case. A cocoa-dependent's brain chemicals only seem to work as a bonding catalyst—the social setting provides the real "psychic Krazy Glue" that makes a given situation (dys)function.

This only follows, considering that the hairiest of all syndromes, i.e., cat-dependence, has as yet no direct chemical link. As the support-group catch phrase has it, "It's not amino acids but the mean old world that makes the difference."

ACTIVITY

As we have noted in this chapter, there are many ways to fall into cat-dependence—all of them bad. Below is a partial list of other dependency support groups that can get you turned around. Join as many as you can, and encourage your friends to join the ones that seem appropriate to their needs. And when you join, tell 'em "Dr." Jeff Reid sent you.

- ☐ Frolic-aholics (play hard, pay hard)
- ☐ Pal-Anon—the group for the person who's everybody's best friend (except his or her own)
- ☐ Slow-Dependents—I think we all know a few of these
- ☐ Deep-End Dependents—anyone who goes over the deep end with their dependencies (I think we all know more than a few of these)
- ☐ Shirkaholic Workaholics—this is the type who spends long hours working at nothing
- ☐ Shop-talkaholics—they always work up to complaining
- ☐ Déjà vu–Dependents—support group for people whose friends complain about the same problems for years without ever attempting to change things

- G.U.Y.S. (Grow Up You Simpletons)—the well-known Men's Hibernation group famous for its weekend getaways (Girls keep out! This is our tree fort!)
- And if all else fails, contact the Association of National Notators of Your Infantile Nagging Gripes—they'll really spell things out for you.

Chapter Eighteen

SCRATCHING POST–MODERNISM: CONTINENTAL LITTER-AREA THEORY CONSIDERED

In theory, anything is possible.

—INSCRIPTION, TOMB OF THE UNKNOWN THEORETICIAN

The French are, *how you say?*, different. So, as you can imagine, in France the whole problem of cat-dependency has been approached in a unique, and rather more theoretical way. Following the French lead, countless continental theorists believe that the breakdown of the distinction between pet and master is symptomatic of a new world (dis)order in which all bets are off and all tenured faculty positions are up for grabs.

In a typically poetic and contrarian mode, French theorists see cat dependence as a sublime form of destruction. They exult in a Dionysian societal breakdown that they've dubbed "scratching post–modernism."

These New Wave scholars inhabit that embattled cultural space where contemporary theories of symbols, symbolism, and symbology confront the runaway train of stagnance, stagnancy, and stagnation. Operating from "the rubble of this intellectual Beirut," as it has been called, they celebrate the "leveling" of the master/pet relationship, arguing that it is symptomatic of the revolutionary "breaking up and breaking down" of contemporary power relations.

Philosopher Michel Furcoat, a leading voice in this continental chorus, asserts that the domestic destruction wreaked by cats is a form of radical commentary on late capitalism (a full treatment of this promising line of research can be surveyed in Furcoat's *Late Capitalism, Early Retirement*). For the French, it would seem, the shredding of interiors is much more than just annoying. In the birthplace of luxury furnishings, such wanton feline destruction becomes a revolutionary gesture of profound signification, an "oppositional rustle of meaning yearning to be heard amidst the din of mass-produced modern hegemony."

Or something like that.

Furcoat argues, for instance, that the way in which cats "deconstruct" a sofa is actually a sophisticated critique of the ossified class structure inherent in modern bourgeois society. "The functionally lumpen-prole pet (read: slave) acts out the latent revolutionary fervor in a semimisdirected act of destruction."

"When Mittens takes her gloves off and gets down to business," he continues, "the inner workings of the Eames chair are laid bare. Armrests are gnawed down to the metal frame. Seat padding, ticking, and springs are tantalizingly revealed by the mercifully brutal claws of our wild sociopolitical sculptor. As much as we may cling to our out-

Scratching Post Modernism: Uneasy Chair Deconstruction

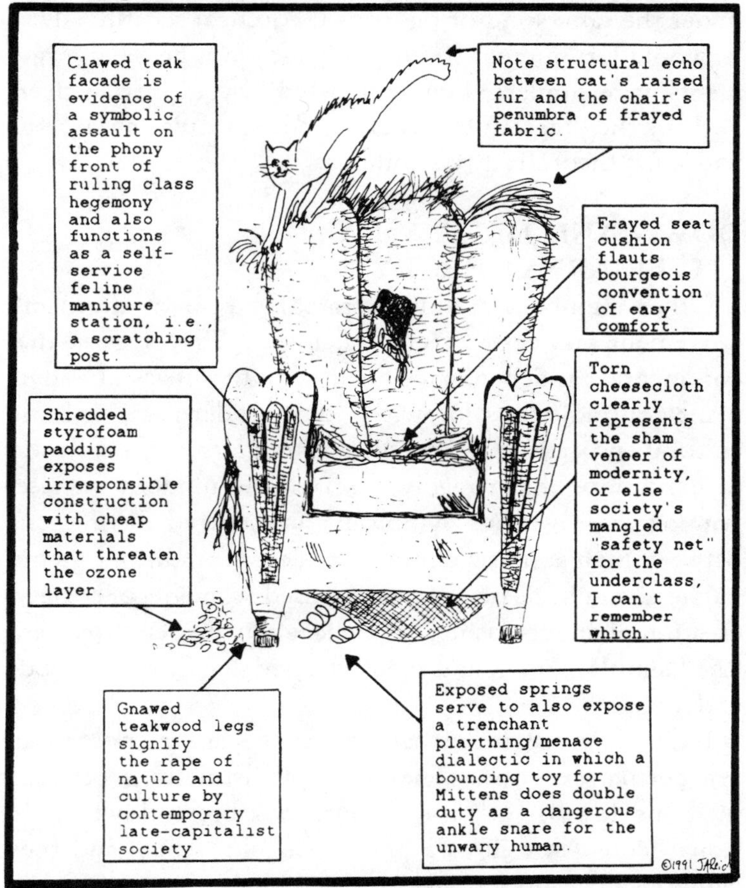

moded notions of *chair-ness* that are hopelessly skewed toward merely pragmatic sit-ability, we must admit that Mittens has made us see the chair in a new, more theoretical way."

The philosopher's notion of understanding via deconstruction is interesting, but I wonder how he'd bear up under the same kind of rigorous theoretical scrutiny. That is, would Dr. Furcoat be best understood if he or his arguments were similarly "deconstructed" by a Siberian tiger? Perhaps the "mercifully brutal" reading would tantalize us with new theoretical possibilities.

DOWN AND DIRTY WITH LITTER-AREA THEORY

Other members of this "scratching post–modernism" movement take less extreme positions. They suggest that continental cat-dependence fits in with that mass of convenient contradictions known as post-modernism. A loose cultural and artistic tendency, post-modernism is a cluster of conditions that roughly describe the modern malaise. Among these various symptoms are blurred distinctions between high and low culture, erosion of traditional genre barriers, emphasis on the marginalized segments of society, creation of an increasingly artificial simulated environment (the "simulacrum"), and the hodgepodging of past periods and styles.

It almost goes without saying that cats are the post-modern pet *par excellence*. They disrupt distinctions between high and low as they leap about, they break down traditional icons (as well as other household items), and they symbolically represent marginalized nature (housed as they are amidst the sanitized simulacrum of contemporary urban existence).

Experience with cats suggests that the post-modern disruptions of the inner life and of contemporary urban apartment life are of a piece. This is where continental "litter-area theory" intersects that realm of "bullshit shoveling" known to specialists as "compost modernism." Litter-area theorists toiling in the field such as Jacques Derriere and Jacques Lickon (known in the theory biz as "the two Jacques") find that when the feline feces hits the fan all sorts of fertile areas for research open up. Needless to say it's a complex scatological interface, and one not easily summarized in a general-interest publication.

Critics of these various continental research avenues suggest that what we're seeing in this welter of theory is nothing more than a highfalutin version of the pathological cat-mirroring behavior we saw in the chapter on "Women Who Love Cats Too Much." There, you'll recall, sufferers of cat-dependency increasingly began to act more feline as the illness progressed. These theorists, too, seem ever more catlike in their argumentation strategies—erratic, eclectic, prone to irrational outbursts, likely to begin spewing incoherent nonsense at unpredictable intervals. And often their pointless, glacially paced pedantry is strongly reminiscent of a cat stalking phantom prey.

In the end, the French contribution to cat-dependency may be negligible due to the philosophical ennui and psychological pessimism that has long made "nothingness" essential to any French philosophical being. Yet ultimately that negative space may give a hint to the moral of this long-winded cautionary tale.

In theory, anything is possible—but nothing is likely.

Chapter Nineteen

HUE AND CRY: WHAT COLOR IS YOUR KITTEN?

The world is a callous hell of colors.

—WALT DIZZY THEME

Color me impressed.

—THE REPLACEMENTS

As humans, all of our perceptions are colored. But the key question is *which* color. Cat-dependents, however, have limited vision in this regard (as in so many others); their view is not so much colored as discolored. They see the world through cat-tainted lenses.

Each individual's choice of "frames," if you will, can give a hint of their predisposition to cat-dependence—and its likely particular manifestations. That is, cat color and breed provide an index to the illness in much the same way that pet names do (see Chapter 7, "What's In? A Name"). As with that Name Game, the choice of cat hue and pedigree are most notable for the "negative space" they carve out, i.e., as pointers to their masters' deep-seated anxieties.

(More shallow-seated anxieties are also sometimes indicated.)

Owners of exotic breeds, for instance, are known to harbor crippling feelings of commonness that induce a sort of plebeian paranoia. They worry that their bloodlines are weaker than their cat's. You often find that a Smith who wishes she was a Smythe owns a Siamese. Conversely, owners of mixed-breed refugees from the alley are more likely to be blue-blooded (yet just as likely to be plunged into the spiritual darkness of cat-dependency).

Cat color schemes present a slightly more complex situation. (For a complete explication of the topics in this chapter, see my earlier book, also titled *What Color Is Your Kitten?*) An increased number of variables and a plethora of personal quirks enter the equation. It's all part of a new kind of "depth analysis" known as chroma-catology, which has been loosely derived from Jungian archetypes. In this system, popular associations for colors combine with deeper psychological triggers to create a network of unique modalities and totalities. It's a heady blend of common sense and uncommon nonsense that ties in surprisingly well with cat-dependence. Some examples:

BLACK TO BASICS

The person who chooses a black cat suffers from one of two (or more) types of basic psychosis. Black is the color of death for most peoples and the person who chooses black might therefore be easily seen as not a "peoples person." This is not necessarily the case, however, inasmuch as the opposite in fact sometimes pertains. Choosing black, therefore, might or might not be a way of whistling in the dark—heading off evil by laughing in its face.

In the case of African-Americans, however, the choice of a black cat evokes a wealth of different associations. One ironic legacy of slavery is that black people are now free to become emotionally shackled to their cats. For this reason, African-Americans who own a black cat may be particularly hesitant to discipline their rogue tom. In a reciprocal racial calculus, a Caucasian person's liberal guilt may promote a lack of cat discipline. But by lowering expectations, cat owners (black and white) actually invite bad behavior.

THE NOT-SO-GREAT WHITE WAY

The choosing of a white cat, of course, is just as rife with racial, psychic, and mythic overtones. The deep insecurities of white supremacists are certainly strongly analogous here. The person who favors a white cat is often psychically compensating for the dark carnival of fear roiling in their unconscious, a cascade of primal shame that siphons all inner joy down a black hole of horror, degradation, and loathing. Or maybe they fear commitment.

In any event, the choice of a noncolor (such as white) is a way to put off till tomorrow what you can't put off till the day after. Some researchers have suggested that those who choose to "go *blanc*" are hiding in the light—which is often the best hiding place of all. You naturally wonder about people who seem so up-front and centered—they must be concealing something awful. It's known as the "Me-Thinks-Thou-Doth-Protest-Too-Much" syndrome, yet not much more is known about it other than its name.

Also, white is the color of mourning for many societies

in the East—which makes the medley of personal and social forces potentially as complicated for white as it is for black.

ANOTHER GRAY AREA

If anything, the choice of a gray cat is even more pathologically noncommittal, making it the classic cat-dependent choice. Fear of commitment is one of the most pronounced symptoms of the syndrome—as if remaining in an eternal holding pattern is better than actually making a choice. People who choose a gray cat often have a simultaneous fear of success and fear of failure. Not to mention a fear of mediocrity.

FOOL'S GOLD

If there's a golden rule when it comes to cats it's that there are no rules, golden or otherwise. Those who choose a golden child for their feline are also inadvertently laying claim to millennia of excess cultural baggage (and needless to say, this often delays cultural deplaning). Given our society's soft spot for blonds and it's plethora of gilded mythologies, the choice is understandable. But, for that very reason, the dashed expectations in this case are likely to be even more crushing for the cat-dependent. When it comes to cats, the golden opportunity is one best passed up.

CALICO-DEPENDENT

The calico presents a special case with its chaotic coat an admixture of melanges mixed with the chaos a "normal" cat creates. The calico owner expects her cat to be all things to all people, but it often turns out to be just a big mix-up.

Calico-Dependent in Denial

THE RED MENACE

"Better dead than red," the reactionaries used to say. But whatever the merits of that statement when it came to the commies, it's not so far off the mark when it comes to kitties. Consider this testimonial from a recovering cat-dependent who had to confront his own quadruped red menace. For the purposes of this book we can call this cat-dependent "Bob," which, ironically, is his name.

"People often say it's always darkest before the dawn," says Bob. "What I want to know is, do these people ever get up early? I mean, it's darkest in the middle of the night, don't kid yourself. I guess I'm getting off the point a little. What I meant to say is that before the dawn, it's red—just like my cat Fireball. I know about the dawn because Fireball wakes me up at all hours. Cats supposedly sleep eighteen hours a day, but how come they're always knocking the waffle iron off the counter at four A.M.?"

Sifting the specific meaning from "Bob's" careening rant isn't easy, but I think it gives some indication of how tough it is "in the red."

ORANGE WITHOUT APPEAL

Orange cats are something wholly other, even more so than other cats. They are like "wholly other" to the nth power. The fact that nothing rhymes with orange, while not really that significant, is in itself an indication of a fundamental incompatibility, albeit only on the level of phonemes. Of course, it runs much deeper than that, extending even to the subterranean linguistic depths of cliché. When things don't belong together, the expression that's always used is that you can't add apples and oranges. Well, eventually, the cat-dependent person with an orange cat discovers that he or she is an apple.

The list of color-coded afflictions could go on and on. There are the telling convict stripes of the Tabby, the S&M foot markings of the dominatrix "Bootsie" or "Mittens" type, the S&L red-handed markings of the cash-and-carry calicos, the fiendish oriental inscrutability of the Siamese and Burmese, the cool occidental detachment of the English Blue (which tends to make the time you own the cat *your* Blue Period). This chroma-catology is a speculative science that's still in its infancy—and like most infants it's got a lot of growing up to do. Yet we can learn a ton from kids, as every mother of a two-year-old will tell you.

ACTIVITY

What color is *your* kitten? If you have more than one cat, do you try to balance their hues? Draw a picture of your cat(s), but color it the way you truly feel. Buy a notebook and record your feelings and images. (Be sure to keep it separate from the notebook journal you purchased for an earlier chapter.) Write and illustrate an essay about your cat's color and the way it makes you feel.

Chapter Twenty

GOING TO THE DOGS: FIFTY WAYS TO LEAVE YOUR ROVER

Love, when not deaf and blind, is sometimes
just plain dumb.

—DOROTHY BARKER

My agent suggested that I call this chapter "I've Gotta Sequel" but for once crasser minds did not prevail. Besides, that might be letting the cat out of the bag before all the chickens have come home to roost, let alone been counted, or—dare I say—hatched. Nonetheless I think it's safe to say that just as cat-dependency is primarily (but not exclusively) a female affair, dog-dependency is mostly a male matter.

The *Cliff's Notes* version of this canine analog of cat-dependency might simply read: Ditto for dogs. But it's never as simple as all that. Indeed, it's symptomatic of this type of mental illness to seek simpleminded answers to such overwhelmingly complex problems. For while there are striking similarities between canine and feline forms of dependency, there are also striking dissimilarities. I could write a book, let me tell you.

Although it's always dangerous to generalize, in general, dependencies on dogs tend to run to the sadistic extreme, whereas cat-dependency—as we have seen—has a strong masochistic bent. Cat-dependency plays into the owner's need for neglect; dog-dependency plays into the owner's need to abuse. Most men can dish it out but they can't take it. For women it's the other way around. A feminist critic might see this as only fitting inasmuch as we're talking about "man's" best friend here—sadism goes hand in paw with patriarchy. You don't have to be Andrea Dworkin to see the sliver of truth in this proposition.

MAN'S INHUMANITY TO MAN'S BEST FRIEND

At any rate, but probably very slowly is best, the dog's guilt-tripping faithfulness is every bit as unhealthy for the putative master as is the cat's snarled psychology. Curiously, dog-dependency brings out the animal in man.

In the popular imagination, the dog is a symbolic underclass icon—sometimes heroic, sometimes not. A few canine clichés serve to bring the point home: it's a dog's life, you've been dogging it, dog days, the underdog, sophomoric doggerel. Even the expression "man's best friend" says more about the attenuation of human friendship than it does about the dog's particular virtue. Of what does this idealized concept of friendship consist? A dog's pronounced "loyalty" is really an inhuman perversion of the human trait. Is it loyalty or stupidity or psychosis that keeps the abused psychically tethered to the abuser?

If the cat's natural essence could be reduced to a political orientation, it would definitely be some sort of atavistic anarchism. Dogs, in the same kind of metaphorical mapping, would be obedient little fascists yapping approval of whatever der führer dictated. But as critics of human slavery long ago noted: slavery deforms the master more than the slave, i.e., it's more damaging to your humanity to enslave others than to be enslaved (though there's little doubt about which one has more fun). A similar situation obtains between the fascist leader and his groveling underlings. In a way, then, the dog plays "the good German shepherd" by following orders and going along to get along; the master becomes a beastly little Hitler.

This only exacerbates interpersonal conflicts, because as pop psychologist E. Costello noted in his influential monograph (stereograph, actually) *Two Little Hitlers:* "Two little Hitlers will fight it out until one little Hitler does the other one's will." In other words, dominance hierarchy tumult will amplify as interpersonal fascism increases. And dog owners, through the playing out of topheavy dominance-submission scenarios with their pets, are increasingly prone to this kind of self-defeating behavior.

NEUROTIC NURTURE VS. PSYCHOTIC NATURE

Characteristically, man becomes his brutish worst in the company of his canine cohort when they go hunting. The dog becomes friendly, earnest, and eager to serve. The man is filled with bloodlust, beer, and B.O. as he bonds with his pals in the great damp outdoors. Conversely, women become meeker and more "civilized" even as their pet cats become increasingly frenzied, i.e., moving toward the wild state. In a spooky symmetry, females' neurotic nurture-mania is mirrored by males' psychotic nature-mania.

Naturally, the same sort of breed analysis can be performed on the canine side of the ledger as we have earlier done on the feline side. It's easy to guess at the hidden anxieties of the man who owns Brutus the snarling Doberman or Fifi the exquisitely coiffed poodle.

The Mysterious Magnetic Properties of Cat Hair

Steve, a dog-dependent who went over the deep end but eventually came back, explains the complex simply as "a power thing, but really a lack-of-power thing." He elaborates: "The dog's natural obsequiousness often brings out the worst in man—we're both herd animals but the human invariably gets to play leader of the pack. Ultimately, however, the dog's deification of the master has unpleasant side effects—absolute power corrupts absolutely, and all that. When a dog will take and take and take abuse (and crawl back for more) the man can get to enjoy doling it out."

This kind of sadistic feedback loop is already well documented even though the study of dog-dependency is in its early phases. Still up in the air is whether canines gain some hidden psychological advantage from their groveling schtick or are merely peddling their loyalty for a lifetime lunch voucher and a warm spot in a comfy chair.

The whole gamut of addiction games, of course, gets played out with Fido, just as it did with Mittens. It almost goes without saying that if there are thirty million vulnerable cat-dependent women out there with lots of disposable income who don't even know (or admit) that they've got a problem, there may be nearly as many "dog-goners" extant among the male population. That's a lot of people who need help. And sad to say we can't help them all. For now, we're going to have to get back and wrap up our volume on cat-dependency. But rest assured, folks, if you just have faith, your dog days are numbered. Even as you read this, we are at work applying and altering the principles of *Cat-Dependent No More* to fit the canine circumstance. It's only a matter of time. And money.

Chapter Twenty-one

ENDING UP AT THE BEGINNING

Getting to the point isn't the point.

—GEORGES SEURAT

How do we begin again? That's the challenge of *Cat-Dependent No More*. But why this question about beginning right near the end? Well, if you've read this book all the way through, and aren't just skimming the ending in a bookstore or at a friend's apartment, you know a little bit about process. *Getting there* isn't the point. Because sometimes, when you get there, there's no "there" there (to borrow Gertrude Stein's appraisal of Los Angeles). We cat-dependents know a thing or two about starting over at the "end," because we do it every day.

Getting there isn't the point. Getting here is. Here and now. Starting over. How do we begin again? In the beginning was the void. And not long after that came avoid. Denial. That's how we got into this mess in the first place.

In other words, it's never really over, yet you must constantly begin again because recovery is the only way out of all those self-destructive cycles. By definition, of course, a cycle is something that repeats, which makes it even tougher. And recovery means you're covering the same ground again. Moreover, as cat-dependents, we've learned the dangers of various holding patterns: holding your own is bad enough, holding someone else's is asking for trouble, holding a cat is the beginning of the end.

And this final chapter is the end of the beginning.

After working your way through this book you should be better equipped to take control of your life. And although there will always be new beginnings, you're now past the initial phase. If you haven't already achieved wellness, you can rest assured that you are well on your way to medium-wellness.

Indeed, after years of working on the problem of cat-dependency I feel barely beyond the initial phase myself. As critical readers may have noticed, my mind still takes the occasional, irrational acrobatic twist of catlike "reasoning." As a result, many of the topics, issues, and slogans that I had initially intended to squeeze into this volume ended up on the cutting-room floor. Yet for all we left out, I know there's plenty that made it in. The general precepts of *Cat-Dependent No More* are of course deceptively simple (where not simply deceptive). And yet like so much else we've learned, they bear repeating.

YOU'VE GOT TO:

- ☐ Stop taking responsibility for the bad behavior of cats (and other "others").
- ☐ Recognize your own reactive personality and stop walking on eggshells.

- ☐ Learn to channel your affections to your fellow humans (because a humane society is a goal for us all, not just a destination for your cat).
- ☐ Try this simple exercise to help you recognize your own cat-dependent behavior: When you find yourself making excuses for your cat's destructive ways, just put a human in Bootsie's shoes and imagine your reaction.

Checklists and hypotheticals are all well and good, but implementing these concepts in specific cases is where things get tricky. This is what we mean when we say, "If you can't come to an understanding, make sure it comes to you." Of course this is difficult if you are suffering from low self-esteem, but you've got to make the best of the situation.

They say that ever since Fulton discovered that low self-esteem is the engine of psychosis, pop psychology has been powered by hot air. While some would say the whole story is apocryphal, I tend to believe that they just made it up. But in any case it doesn't really matter. What really matters is the story's resonance, and to a lesser extent its timbre.

So it is with cat-dependence. What's important is not "the letter" of the flaw, but the spirit of this sickness. If, as some naysayers say, cat-dependence is only an imaginary mental illness, then in a sense it's merely semantic—either way it's all in your head. But we've all come too far, and made too much progress (whether real or imagined), for this to be just another head trip.

Because, as everyone knows, when you trip you often come crashing down. And after a big fall, it's tougher than ever to get back up again—just ask Humpty Dumpty. It's much better to keep it all under control and keep it all together. As the Chinese proverb has it, "The greatest journey begins with a single step." Similarly, the momentous trail away from cat-dependency starts with Nine Steps, one after another. And if there's no better way to begin than with a single step, I can think of no better way to end *Cat-Dependent No More* than with the Nine Steps. Remember: Easy doesn't.

NINE STEPS TO START LIVING YOUR OWN NINE LIVES

1) We admit that we are powerless—our cats have become unmanageable.
2) Ask someone higher (or at least taller) than ourselves what to do.
3) Ask him to grant us the serenity to prioritize our inventories and take an inventory of our priorities. Or vice versa.
4) Talk to our friends about ourselves and our problems until *they* are blue in the face.
5) Repeat one of the previous steps while we stall for time.
6) Remember that "act" all mixed up is "cat."
7) Realize that getting the kitten off your back requires an understanding that sometimes the softest things are also the hardest.
8) Recognize that where there's a cat, there's a catch.
9) Having first purchased this book for ourselves, we will now purchase it for someone else.